Jean-Baptiste Berthier

States of the Christian Life and Vacation

Jean-Baptiste Berthier

States of the Christian Life and Vacation

ISBN/EAN: 9783743369153

Manufactured in Europe, USA, Canada, Australia, Japa

Cover: Foto ©Lupo / pixelio.de

Manufactured and distributed by brebook publishing software (www.brebook.com)

Jean-Baptiste Berthier

States of the Christian Life and Vacation

STATES

OF

THE CHRISTIAN LIFE

AND

VOCATION,

ACCORDING TO THE DOCTORS AND THEOLOGIANS OF THE CHURCH.

BY

REV. J. BERTHIER,

MISSIONER OF OUR LADY OF LA SALETTE.

PREFACE BY REV. JOSEPH SHEA, S. J.

WITH THE APPROBATION OF

THE MASTER OF THE SACRED PALACE, AND OF HIS EMINENCE,
CARDINAL McCLOSKEY.

NEW YORK:
P. O'SHEA, 37 BARCLAY STREET.
1879.

Copyright, P. O'SHEA, 1879.

Stereotyped and printed at the
BOYS' PROTECTORY,
West Chester, New York.

PREFACE.

The few years that make up what is called a man's life, are of the utmost importance. They determine his entire eternity. Our Father in Heaven takes a deep interest in them, and does not wish them to be a failure. On our part, then, we should not misuse these years, and much less should we trifle them away. A pagan emperor mourned the loss even of one day. St. Paul tells us (Gal. vi, 10) that all our time is given to us to work good.

The proper way, therefore, for us to live, is to do God's ever-holy will in this world; to embrace that state and form of life which Divine Providence has traced out for us. When we live where God wants us to be, graces are proportioned to difficulties, and the current of life flows on as smoothly as we can expect it to do in our present condition.

The little work, of which we here present a translation, teaches us admirably how to follow and carry out the guidance of God during our sojourn on this earth. The original has been highly commended by several French bishops. It was published with the approbation of the Master of the Sacred Palace. It even merited for its learned author a most complimentary letter from the immortal Pius IX.

Father Berthier's teaching is drawn from the most reliable Catholic sources. We are not astonished that his work has gone through several editions in France. We hope that the same success awaits it in its English dress. In all probability, this translation is not what it could be in abler hands; but any defect in that line cannot detract from the intrinsic worth of the book itself. In our humble opinion, Father Berthier has given us one of the best, if not the very best, of books, upon the grave subject of vocation.

We trust that this modest translation will be instrumental in spreading more correct views on the Christian Life, and in preventing many from rushing into a state of life from unworthy motives, and especially without consulting God. Father Berthier's book will be a light to the clergy and the laity; for it will put the various states clearly before the mind of the latter, and enable the former to be good guides for those who ask their advice when there is question of making a choice.

INTRODUCTION.

Every one understands the importance of the question of vocation. Souls that are not removed from the influence exercised by religious indifference and the prejudices of the world, acknowledge that, on the choice of a state, depends the happiness or misfortune of life. Parents who reflect are, with reason, anxious about the calling of their children; and every director of souls is aware that one cannot, without danger, overlook, in this important matter, the rules of Christian wisdom.

But where are these rules laid down? Where can one get an accurate idea of them? Evidently, it is not in the maxims of the world, but in Holy Writ, in Catholic tradition, in the works of the fathers, and in the theologians and masters of the spiritual life. And yet, where is the young man or the young woman, who, having to decide about the future, can run over immense volumes, written, for the most part, in an unknown tongue, with a view to draw from them the doctrine that is to enlighten and guide a decision? Absorbed as they are in countless occupations, parents are still less fit than their children for such a study. Hardly, even, will the duties of the ministry allow priests leisure enough to explore the fathers and doctors so as to fathom a subject over which prejudices, accumulated by the spirit of the world and revolutions, have flung such a vast amount of darkness. To make serious researches, then, in the works of the great masters, to gather their teachings into one volume that every one can read, has appeared to us a useful task. This was the reason that led us to undertake it. Our purpose, in this book, is not to exhort souls to this or that state of life. We do not even wish to protest against certain views which, to us, seem at variance with true doctrine, and still pass current in the times in which we live. All we aim at is conscientiously to state what we consider to be the truth.

"Our doctrine is not ours," we would venture to say with the Saviour: it is that of the Scriptures, of the fathers, and of theologians.

The Epistles of St. Paul, commented by the learned Cornelius à Lapide; the doctors of the Church, and, chiefly, St. John Chrysostom, who, in the words of Bossuet, is inferior to none in good sense and eloquence; St. Jerome, who, having read every author, summed up, so to say, in himself the testimony of all, as well as of universal tradition; * St. Augustine, called by St. Isidore the Master, next to St. Paul, of the Church; † St. Thomas, who, according to a great pope, wrought as many miracles as he wrote articles; ‡ St. Liguori, whose doctrine, according to the declarations of the Holy See, every confessor can follow with a safe conscience; among theologians, Suarez, whose profound learning and great authority no one will contest; Sanchez, whom St. Liguori styled very pious and wise; § Lessius, praised by St. Francis of Sales; St. Ignatius of Loyola, whose exercises have always been so much esteemed by popes and all the children of the Church; finally, F. Pinamonti, whom St. Liguori quotes:—these are the sources from which we draw our teaching. They are rich, and, hence, we have taken largely from them; and the more so, that, in a question of such weight, we did not like to say anything of our own.

If, then, while perusing these pages, the reader should chance to fall on a view hitherto unknown to him, let him not, on that account, be in a hurry to blame it. Let him have the goodness to weigh the reasons and authority of the theologian who holds it; and not condemn our humble work without hearing it, that is, without

---

* *Défense de la tradition des pères.* † Ibid:
‡ John XXII, J'Abbé Drioux. introd. à la Somme, p. 10.
§ St. Lig., l. iv, n. 478, ed. Mellier.

reading it from beginning to end. It is not from the reading of a single chapter that a book can be judged. In the matter of which we now treat, everything is linked. The second part cannot be understood unless the first has been studied.

When we entered on our researches, we ourselves were surprised to find in St. Thomas, but chiefly in St. Liguori, doctrines altogether contrary to our previous views on vocation. In presence of such authorities, it gave us no pain to put aside our own thoughts. Doubtless, our readers will act in like manner, should they find themselves in a similar position. Better regulate our method of judging and acting by the teachings of those who are our masters and guides, than follow the daring road traced out by a pretended experience or personal views.

Every one may verify the exactness of our quotations, for we point out with scrupulous care the sources from which we derive them. Notwithstanding the reliability of the teaching of these theologians whom we cite, despite all the pains we have been at not to wander from their doctrine, we wished, and have obtained, that our work should be examined by the Papal Censors, and that its publication should have the sanction of the very reverend Master of the Sacred Palace. The first edition that appeared was printed at the press of the Sacred Congregation of the Propaganda, in Rome during the month of May, 1874. The edition which we now issue, entirely coincides with the first.*

Here is the order that we have followed. In the first part, we treat of the states of Christian life so as to furnish an exact notion of them; in the second, we discuss the choice of a state of life and vocation.

---

* We have suppressed some theological opinions which appeared to us above the reach of the general reader.

JOHN M. KELLY LIBRARY

Donated by
**The Redemptorists of
the Toronto Province**
from the Library Collection of
Holy Redeemer College, Windsor

University of
St. Michael's College, Toronto

CONTENTS.

	PAGE.
PREFACE,	iii
INTRODUCTION,	v

PART I.

STATES OF THE CHRISTIAN LIFE.

PRELIMINARY EXPLANATIONS.

	PAGE.
Section I.—The Common State of Life,	4
Article I.—Marriage,	6

CHAPTER I.
Is Marriage a Holy State,	8

CHAPTER II.
Is Marriage Obligatory,	14

CHAPTER III.
Is Marriage counselled,	19

CHAPTER IV.
End to be kept in View by those entering the Married State,	25

CHAPTER V.
Chief Cases in which Marriage is Unlawful or Invalid,	30
Article II.—The Unmarried State,	33
Paragraph I.—Celibacy,	34

CHAPTER I.

Is Episcopacy the Most Perfect State of the Christian Life, - 201

CHAPTER II.

Is the State of Priests having Charge of Souls More Perfect than the Religious State, - - - - - - 206

CHAPTER III.

What are the Signs and Conditions of a Vocation to Holy Orders, - - - - - - - - - - 213

PART II.

THE CHOICE OF A STATE OF LIFE AND VOCATION.

Section I.—Means to know what State of Life we should choose, - - - - - - - - - - 226

CHAPTER I.

Prayer, - - - - - - - - - - 227

CHAPTER II.

Reflection, - - - - - - - - - 232

CHAPTER III.

Consultation, - - - - - - - - - 240

Section II.—Rules to be followed in choosing a State of Life, 246

CHAPTER I.

Rules to be followed when a State is Obligatory, - - 247

CHAPTER II.

Rules when a Religious Vocation is Doubtful, - - - 253

CHAPTER III.

Rules when those about to choose a State have not even a Doubtful Vocation for the Religious Life, - - - 265

CHAPTER IV.

Rules to discover what is Most Pleasing to God, when a Person is Free to choose the State which he thinks Proper for himself, - - - - - - - - - 269

CHAPTER V.

Three Times Suitable for making a Right Choice, - - - 274

CHAPTER VI.

How to act after an Election, - - - - - - 282
Conclusion, - - - - - - - - - 291
Prayers, - - - - - - - - 291

FIRST PART.

STATES OF THE CHRISTIAN LIFE.

PRELIMINARY EXPLANATIONS.

WHAT IS MEANT BY STATES OF CHRISTIAN LIFE: HOW MANY THERE ARE.

Suarez defines, as follows, a state of Christian life: "It is a stable and fixed manner of living, established to preserve grace in this world, and to obtain glory in the world to come."*

" Between the Church of Christ yet militant on earth, and the Church triumphing in heaven, there exists such a wondrous harmony, that, in the Gospels, the Church of the earth is often called the kingdom of heaven. As, in the Church of heaven, there are many classes of blessed spirits to carry out the orders of God and encircle his throne, so, in the Church on earth, there are

---

* Lib. i, *De statu perfectionis*, c. ii, n. 7. Whenever we quote Suarez we refer to his 7th treatise, "*De religione, de obligationibus quæ religiosum statum constituunt vel ad illum disponunt.*" In giving the doctrine of fathers and theologians, our aim is to render faithfully their teachings, rather than to give a word-for-word translation.

various analogous degrees. And, just as in the perfection of the essential blessedness of the elect there are divers states, with much variety in glory and accidental rewards, in like manner, there must be, in the militant Church, several states in which men may fit themselves for varying degrees of happiness, and may merit honors and recompenses of different kinds. In the heavenly country, this variety clothes the society of the elect with admirable beauty, and the Church of Christ here below derives ravishing splendor from the diversity of states.

"This is what the Psalmist sung (Ps. xliv): 'The queen stood on thy right hand . . . surrounded with variety. . . . All the glory of the king's daughter is within in golden borders, clothed round about with varieties.'" *

"The states of the Christian are divided into the common and the perfect. And, indeed, as we have just remarked, a state of Christian life is a fixed and stable manner of living, instituted and ordained for the preservation of grace at present, and for glory hereafter. But this manner of living is twofold. One manner is general and common to all the faithful, since it is necessary for salvation, and God wishes all to be saved. The other is special. In addition to these means of salvation which are necessary, it possesses many others. These two manners of living. . .

---

*Suar., ibid., c. ii, n. 6.

form two different states of Christian life: the common state, and the state of perfection." *

"Though the former state is called *common*, it does not mean that those who live in it may not perform works of supererogation, and are incapable of growing, with the assistance of God's grace, in spiritual perfection as much as they choose; but it is so called, because that state does not bind its members to supererogatory works and perfection, nor does it afford them any special means for that purpose.

"The state of perfection adds something better and more perfect to the common state, and is thereby distinguished from it, as the container differs from what it contains." †

"In the state of perfection there are more means to practise virtue, and fewer occasions to violate God's law; wherefore we find in it greater utility and fuller security." ‡

"This division which we have just given of the Christian life is not only excellent and necessary, but is furthermore complete; for we cannot imagine any state among the children of the Church which it does not cover."§

Now, then, we shall enter into some details, first, on common life, and, next, on the state of perfection; not for the purpose of treating the

---

* Suarez, c. ii, n. 7.
† *Tanquam includens ab incluso.* (Ibid., c. ii, n. 9.)
‡ Ibid., c. ii, n. 10.   § Ibid., c. ii, n. 12.

question exhaustively, but to convey an exact idea of the two states to those who have to make or to direct a choice of life.

We write, chiefly, with a view to enlighten persons who have to embrace a state, whatever may be their age or their sex.

SECTION I.—THE COMMON STATE OF LIFE.

We shall include in this state every one who is not in the perfect state, specially so called; that is, all who are not in the religious state, or have not been raised to the episcopate.* Indeed the common state of life contains many classes of human beings who, although in conditions otherwise differing, are in the same state with respect to the Christian life. Above all, we must declare that it does not enter into our purpose to judge of or compare the interior state of the souls that are in divers positions, "for man seeth the things that appear, but the Lord beholds the heart." (1 Kings xvi, 7.) Suarez, following St. Thomas, says: "There is nothing to hinder a man from being perfect, even though he has not embraced a state of perfection. It may also happen that one who is in a state of perfection is not perfect. These two propositions are beyond doubt, and supported by experience. All religious are in a

---

* We shall speak on vocation to the priesthood when we come to treat of the state of perfection in exercise.

perfect state, and still not all are perfect; some of them may not be even in a state of grace. On the other hand, many seculars and married people may be perfect, though, for all that, not in a state of perfection. The reason or proof of the first proposition is, that we can contract an obligation and not comply with it; have an employment and neglect it. . . . Even when in a perfect state, man always remains free to acquire, or not to acquire, perfection." *

"The proof of the second proposition is, that, though the state of perfection facilitates the acquirement of perfection, nevertheless it is not a necessary means to acquire it. To reach perfection, the soul need not keep all the counsels: it is enough to keep some of them; and we can, even when not in a state of perfection, perform works of counsel, and thus spontaneously arrive at perfection." †

It were, then, imprudent and rash to measure the interior perfection of souls by the state in which they live. Following the great theologians and doctors, we can study and compare the exterior states of life that are in the Church, and whose variety is one of the many beauties of the Spouse of Christ. But, in this study and comparison, we must be careful not to swerve from the doctrine of those who are our guides

---

* Suarez, *De statu perfectionis*, c. v, n. 1. S. Th., ii, 2, q. 184, a. 4.
† Ibid., c. v, n. 2.

and our masters. To act otherwise would be to expose ourselves to go astray and fall into error. Do we not hear—too often, alas!—Christians, who, without knowing it, talk of the various states of Christian life, just as do heretics upon whom the Church has set her anathema?

ARTICLE I.

Marriage.

Let us open this subject with the grave and remarkable words of the catechism of the Council of Trent, whose high authority no one will call into question: " Since the pastors of souls ought always to have in view the happy and perfect life of Christians, they should wish, above all, what the apostle wished for himself. Writing to the Corinthians, he says to them : ' I wish that all men were like myself:' namely: that all should practise continence, or perfect chastity. Indeed, the most blessed thing for a Christian in this life is, to have his mind free from all the distractions and solicitudes of the world, to reign over his passions, subdued, and almost extinct, through virtue, and to repose blissfully in the practice of piety and in holy thoughts of heaven.

" But, as marriage has been enriched by God with a multitude of gifts, . . . it is clear that the faithful should be instructed in what relates to that state."* This is what we are about to do. Marriage is the conjugal, legitimate, and indissoluble union of man and woman, raised by our Lord to the dignity of a sacrament.

"Jesus Christ himself merited for us, by his passion, the grace which sanctifies spouses, perfects their mutual love, and strengthens the indissolubility of their union."† "If any one says that marriage is not, truly and properly, one of the seven sacraments of the New Law, and that it does not confer grace, let him be anathema."‡ Thus the Church speaks through the holy Council of Trent.

On the subject of marriage, we shall answer only the following questions, which appear to us best to suit our purpose:—1. Is marriage a holy state? 2. Is it obligatory? 3. Is it counselled? 4. What ends should be had in view by those who enter it? 5. What are the chief cases in which marriage is unlawful or invalid?

---

* *Catechismus ad parochos, de matrimonio,* n. 1.
† Council of Trent, sess. 24.
‡ Ibid., sess. 24, can. 1.

CHAPTER I.

IS MARRIAGE A HOLY STATE.

St. Paul says: "He that giveth his virgin in marriage doth well;" and, "If thou take a wife, thou hast not sinned." (1 Cor. vii, 38, 28.) In spite of this distinct declaration of the apostle, some heretics of the first ages, the Manicheans among others, condemned marriage, and were themselves in turn condemned by the fathers of the Church. Among the foremost, St. John Chrysostom eloquently lays down the Catholic doctrine on this head:—

"We consider marriage lawful; we also admire those who forego it. To keep from what is forbidden does not always betoken a grand and lofty soul. Hence, perfect virtue, not content with shunning faults branded by public opinion, triumphs in the performance of those acts, the omission of which would entail no guilt. But do you not prohibit marriage? God forbid! But, you will add, do you exhort us to keep continence? Yes, I advise it, for I understand the excellence of virginity; still, far from censuring marriage as being bad, I praise it. . . .

Yet you will grant that there are Christians to whom this assistance is of no use. These are the persons whom I invite to embrace virginity, without, however, condemning marriage. Now, between counsel and prohibition, there lies an abyss as deep as between liberty and necessity. A friend who counsels, leaves his friend free to follow another view.

"When I advise virginity, I pass no censure on marriage; nor do I blame him who resists my counsels. I admire, indeed, the generous athlete who rushes on in the career of virginity, but I have no fault to find with him who does not enter that career: for blame is allowed only in reference to a really bad act. But how can it attach to a Christian whose only reproach is, that he confines himself within a more modest sphere, and dares not aim at the highest efforts of virtue? I shall not, indeed, praise the vigor and energy of his courage; but neither shall I allow myself to cast blame on timid reserve. I do not, then, oppose marriage, which I hold to be holy and lawful; I condemn only those who outrage and profane it.

"Thus it is that Catholic doctrine knows how to venerate the work of God, and give additional splendor to the honor and glory of virginity. The value is very doubtful of a good which passes for such, only when compared with some great evil. A good that is truly great is one which is above what all the world agrees to look upon as good. Our doctrine ... proclaims marriage to be good, and virginity better. To call marriage bad, is an injury to virginity; to honor the former, is to praise the latter. A person is not handsome because less ugly than some one else whose body is deformed; but he is truly such, when he excels in beauty those who are whole and free from defect. In this way, marriage, which is good in itself, leads us to admire virginity, that is better, and outstrips it in dignity as much as the captain and the general are above the common soldier and sailor."*

"Marriage is good, since it keeps man to his duty, and hinders him from falling into sin Therefore, do not condemn it, because it is fruitfu. in happy results. It saves us from profaning the holy temple of our body; it supports the weak, and strengthens their steps. But a support of that kind is of no use to the strong and robust man. Far from being necessary for him, its sole effect is to scatter in his way a thousand obstacles which slacken his progress, while lessening his merit and glory."†

The Angelic Doctor develops still better, and with more precision, the advantages of marriage. He adds three others to the one instanced by St. Chrysostom, namely: children, fidelity, and

---

* S. J. Chrysost., *De virginitate*, c. 8-10. Ed. Migne.
† Ibid., c. xxv.

the sacraments.* The catechism of the Council of Trent explains those three advantages of marriage. The first consists in children born of a lawful wife. St. Paul sets so high a value on this first benefit, that he writes: " She shall be saved through childbearing." (1 Tim. ii, 15.) The meaning of these words of the apostle must not be restricted to mean physical generation; it takes in, also, education and zeal in forming children to piety. The second benefit is the fidelity that mutually binds husband and wife, one to the other, whereby they give one another a right which they pledge themselves never to violate. The third is the sacrament, to wit: the bond of wedlock, which cannot be loosened.†

" The birth of children, fidelity, and the sacraments," continues St. Thomas, " not only palliate marriage, but render it even holy."‡ We gather from all this what ought to be the dispositions of those who enter the married state. They should consider themselves as undertaking not a human, but a divine work, to which they ought to bring great purity of heart and piety; as the examples given by the ancient patriarchs of the Old Law abundantly show. Although the marriage of these holy men did not bear the character of a sacrament, they themselves, however, always

---

* Supplem., q. 49, a. 2.
† *Catech. Conc. Trid. de matrim.*, 30.
‡ Supplem., q. 49, a. 4.

looked upon that solemn act as requiring a deep sense of religion and great piety for its due performance.*

Who does not know that, as marriage is a sacrament of the living, it were a sacrilege to receive it except in the state of grace? For this reason the faithful consider it a duty to prepare for it by going to confession. Woe to those who, on such an occasion, would confess their sins from a mere religious formalism, and not with the candor and repentance which justify before God. The blessing imparted by the priest to such a marriage would turn into a curse that would weigh upon the entire after-life of the contracting parties. And woe, likewise, to those who, before entering this state, allow themselves intimacies that are dangerous, when they are not culpable. These rash people forget the simplest rules of Christian prudence; carry on, alone, conversations and familiarities, which St. Jerome calls the beginning of the agony of virtue. "Never," says this great doctor to Nepotian,—" never sit alone together, without a witness to your words and actions."† Experience testifies that this wise counsel cannot be neglected without danger. When passion alone unites a pair, it soon divides them. We see, not unfrequently, a life of discord and hatred following close upon intimacies alarming to purity. In this way, the justice of God

---

* Catech., ibid., 36. † Epist. ad Nepotian. 5.

falls, even in this world, on those who offend it. And this same justice will not spare those parents, those blind and guilty masters, who, by their negligence, have made themselves the accomplices of the moral waywardness of their children and servants.

CHAPTER II.

IS MARRIAGE OBLIGATORY.

According to Suarez, marriage was, by natural right, binding on our first parents after their fall; but this obligation held good only for the case of necessity to propagate and sustain the human race, as the precept of almsgiving urges only when the needs of some individuals demand it.* "It is difficult for me to admit," continues this great theologian, "that, after the days of our first parents, there ever was a time when this law was imperative for all men, or even for any one of them in particular. For, as soon as the need ceased, the obligation must also have come to an end; or, if it lasted beyond that, it could not do so for a long time. I have, therefore, demonstrated, from Scripture and the fathers, that in the Old Law there was, with regard to marriage, no command binding all men; and I have shown that many holy persons led a single life: which is proof that celibacy was not forbidden. It is very likely that among the heathens many, even before the Mosaic dispensation, abstained from marriage, and were never blamed for so doing by the philo-

---

* Suarez, *De voto castitatis*, c. i, n. 6.

sophers and historians of best repute. In those times, therefore, marriage was not considered obligatory; and if, then, there existed no obligation in regard to it, we have now far greater evidence that it does not bind under the law of grace."*

"At present," says the catechism of the Council of Trent, "since the human race is sufficiently multiplied, not only there is no command ordaining marriage, but virginity is highly recommended and counselled to *every one* in Holy Writ."†

Suarez confesses that marriage is necessary in the Church of Christ for the preservation of the human race.‡ But it does not follow that any individual, taken separately, is bound to enter that state; otherwise, as St. Thomas observes, we should say, for a like reason, that an individual man is bound to engage in agriculture, to be a mason, or to follow some other of the various trades which are indispensable for society.§

"Human nature," adds the same great doctor, "inclines one man to one employment, and another to a different one, according to the diversities of individual character. Through this diversity, combined with the providence of God, which moderates all things, one man embraces this condition of life,—agriculture, for instance,

---

* Suar., *De voto castitatis*, lib. 9, c. i, n. 7.
† Catech. Conc. Trid. de matrim., 14.
‡ Suar., *De statu perfectionis*, lib. I, c. ii, n. 14.
§ St. Th., *Supplem.*, q. 41, a. 2.

while another follows something quite different. In precisely the same way, some adopt marriage, and others devote themselves to a contemplative life, without any danger to society."

"Some rare cases may present themselves," says Suarez, "in which, for the sake of peace, the conversion of a country to the faith, or some other similar public good, a person may, from charity, have a duty to get married."* Mark well, that there is question here of the temporal or spiritual good of an entire country; not merely of the good of a single individual. According to Sanchez, whom St. Liguori styles very wise and pious, and according to St. Liguori himself, a man who has dishonored a young woman under promise of marriage, is bound to marry her.†

"I cannot admit," says Suarez, "that a man can be in such a moral danger of falling into sins against chastity as to be obliged to matrimony in order to avoid them; for, to shun occasions and overcome temptations, he always has the means supplied by prayer, fasting, and other remedies of that nature."‡ On this point St. Liguori professes the same doctrine as Suarez. In his mind, the man who, from frequent falls, has had experience of his own weakness, would be obliged to get married, in case he would not

---

* Suar., *De voto castitatis*, lib. 9, c. ii, n. 7.
† St. Lig., *Theol. Mor.*, lib. 3, tr. 2, n. 209, ed. Taurin. Sanch., *De s. matrim.*, lib. 1, Disp. 4.
‡ Suarez, ibid., c. ii, n. 8.

take other means to avoid a relapse; but there is no one, provided he wills sincerely, that cannot use salutary remedies for his cure. For, who is there that has not, under his hands, the powerful arm of prayer, with which every passion can be conquered?*

This doctrine of the great saint condemns such as make no effort to throw off their sinful habits, expose themselves thoughtlessly to every kind of danger, neglect to ask God through the sacraments and prayer, the assistance of which is indispensable for them, and still keep away from marriage, so as to lead, with greater freedom, a disorderly life.

This is the place for the question which St. Liguori puts: "Is a child bound to obey his parents who order him or her to marry?" The holy doctor answers: "The common opinion is that the child is not obliged." He then quotes another theologian, whose teaching he prefers: "All that a parent is allowed to do here is to request his child to marry for some just cause, such as the preservation of the family." In the same place, the saint brings forward another authority that says: "A parent can in nowise force his child to marry who has a desire to enter a better state; that is to say, religious life or celibacy."†

---

* St. Lig., *Theol. Mor.*, lib. 3, tr. 2, n. 209.
† Ibid., lib. 6, tr. 6, n. 850.

With the exception, then, of rare cases, no one is bound to marry. "He that giveth her not" (his daughter in marriage), "doth better," says the apostle (1 Cor. vii, 38), "than he that giveth." These last words are St. Thomas' commentary, who adds: "No one has a right to a reward for transgressing a precept." Now, a special reward, namely, the aureola, or halo, is due to virgins: therefore, marriage is not compulsory.

CHAPTER III.

IS MARRIAGE COUNSELLED

The word "counsel" may have two meanings: the one broad, the other precise and restricted. "Taken in a broad sense, counsel may apply even to commands," says Suarez. Every day we counsel ourselves and others to keep the commandments; and God counsels the same by continual inspirations, and even exhortations, such as are to be found in the sacred writings.* In this sense we advise marriage in the few cases in which it is obligatory; and those who fall within these cases may validly bind themselves by vow to marry, though such a vow is usually null, as not having for object a good greater than the one it removes: for celibacy, in itself, is better than wedlock.† "Still," continues Suarez, "in a precise and rigorous sense, the counsel that God gives with respect to certain good works has no precept in view, but only what is not commanded. Every good work not commanded is not thereby a matter of counsel."‡ It must, besides, surpass

---

* Suar., *De statu perf.*, lib. I, c. vii, n. 6.
† St. Liguori, *Theol. Moral.*, lib. 3, tr. 2, n. 209. Sanchez, *De matrim.*, lib. I, Disp. 4.   ‡ Suar., ibid.

in goodness the opposite work, which cannot be performed simultaneously with itself. He who gives his daughter in marriage does well, but he who does not give her does better, says the great apostle. Virginity is then counselled, because it is opposed to marriage, and better than it. Among actions not commanded there are some that are simply good, but in a lower degree: such is marriage. As all hold this view to be certain, marriage is not among the counsels.* Hence, St. Liguori wrote as follows to a young man who consulted him about his vocation: "As to the married state, I cannot counsel it you, since St. Paul does not counsel it to any one, unless there is a necessity from habitual faults: which, I am confident, is not your case." The holy doctor, as remarkable for his piety as for his great experience and vast erudition, wrote in the same spirit, and almost in the same words, to a young lady, who had asked him for light.† St. Paul, under divine inspiration, wrote: "If they do not contain themselves" (*i. e.*, cannot observe chastity), "let them marry. For it is better to marry than to be burnt"—by the fires of temptation. (1 Cor. vii, 9.) "Remember," says the learned commentator, Cornelius à Lapide, "that to be burnt does not mean to be tempted, but to give way to the tempter."‡ On these words of St. Paul, St.

---

* *Non est opus consilii, ut apud omnes constat.* Suar., ibid., lib. 1, c. vii, nn. 6, 7. † S. Liguori, *Œuvres ascétiques*, ad Casterman, t. 3, pp. 503 et 511.   ‡ In loco.

Augustine, in a book published for the special purpose of defending marriage against heretics who assailed its holiness, writes: " It appears to me that, in these times (under the law of grace,) only those who cannot observe chastity ought to marry."*

Even for those in such a condition, marriage is strictly obligatory only in so far as they do not wish to take other means against relapses, as we have previously stated.

After noting that the passage of St. Paul, to which St. Augustine alludes, is applicable to those only who have not vowed chastity, as the context manifestly proves, Suarez goes on to say: " The apostle does not assert that it is better to marry than to keep continency, for continency is better; but he asserts that it is better to marry than to fall into sin; so that, absolutely, he counsels continency as better, and declares without restriction: ' I wish that all men were like me;' but he sets marriage before sin."† However, as the eminent theologian pursues, men can always, with the help of divine grace, refrain from both—marriage and sin—and do what is better than either of them, to wit, " observe complete chastity."‡ Since then, according to Suarez, the apostle counsels celibacy

---

* St. Aug., *De bono conjugii*, c. x: "*Mihi videtur hoc tempore solos eos qui se non continent conjugari oportere.*" In c. ix, *De sancta virginitate*, he says: "*Nunc autem . . . ea tantum quæ se non continet nubat.*" Ed. Migne, c. 400.

† Suar., *De voto cast.*, lib. 9, c. ii, n. 8; et I Cor. vii, 7.

‡ Ibid.

as the better, marriage, its opposite, is not of counsel in the strict sense of the word.

Doctrine like this should, it seems, influence the conduct of parents, and of all whose state may cause them to be consulted on a vocation. Cornelius à Lapide relates that St. Augustine, like St. Ambrose, would never advise any one to marry.

In his life of the great doctor, Possidonius tells us that he recommended a pious man to observe three things: first, never to seek a wife for any one, for fear that, after marriage, the couple would curse him that brought them together.* We make no mention of the other two points, because they do not concern our subject.

In presence of such teaching and such examples, have we not reason to wonder when virtuous young people of both sexes receive, without any reason, and in a tone of authority, from parents, in other respects Christian, or from others, decisions like this: "You are called to the married state: it is God's will that you enter it"? We suppose that these young persons do not come under any of the cases wherein marriage is binding, nor even under the case of which there is question in the passage quoted above from St. Liguori. We ask what is to be understood by that pretended vocation to the married state, so peremptorily decided on, which would impose upon the young persons in question an obligation of conscience

---

* Corn. in 1 Cor. vii, 28.

to contract marriage? Is that vocation commanded? Then, what commandment of God or Church ordains it? Can it be only a counsel? But have we not just seen that, according to St Liguori, the apostle counsels marriage to none save those afflicted with guilty habits? Even supposing such habits, " who ever pretended that marriage is an essential means to guard against sin?"* says the same holy doctor. Are we to forget that, in times wherein practical faith is often wanting, and, at least, one of the spouses may disregard it altogether, marriage is not always a sure preservative against temptations and relapses? Is there not, in many cases, reason to inquire whether there be not some other remedy for human frailty more efficacious than marriage contracted in certain conditions? Once more, what is this vocation? Is it, perhaps, a natural inclination? Marriage being a holy state, it is ordinarily allowable to follow such an inclination, provided a virtuous end is kept in view. But, can it be said that inclination to marriage, even when joined with aptitude for the state, is such a mark of divine vocation as to entail obligation? Can it be inferred that the person experiencing an inclination of this nature would do better by entering the married state, than by choosing a more perfect life, and triumphing, through virtue, over natural tastes and leanings?

---

* St. Lig., *Theol. Mor.*, lib. 6, n. 75.

Have all who live happily in virginity or the religious life resisted grace, and perchance missed their vocation, because, though fit for marriage, they felt, at certain times in their lives, a leaning which they put away as a temptation? Who does not see that aptitude and inclination for marriage do not prove any more a supernatural call to that state, than the appetite and vigorous stomach of a man are evidence that God does not wish him to fast or mortify his tastes. To explain, then, and to justify decisions of this sort, we must suppose an inspiration or a revelation of the Holy Ghost. But, we may well ask, is it easy to believe in a divine inspiration impelling in a way contrary to evangelical counsels?

Let us keep before our eyes the following saying of St. Ignatius of Loyola: "More signs are required to decide that God intends a man to remain in a state wherein the observance of the commandments alone suffices, than to believe the same man to be called to the practice of evangelical counsels; for our Lord openly exhorts us to follow these counsels." *

---

* *Directorium*, c. xxii, n. 4.

CHAPTER IV.

END TO BE KEPT IN VIEW BY THOSE ENTERING THE MARRIED STATE.

"It is no harm to wish marriage," says Suarez; and he adds: "I confess, however, that the desire for marriage is not good merely for its object; we must, besides, look to the end for which we wish it; we must consider the motives that give rise to that desire."*

It would be criminal to enter that state while putting aside its essential end, or with the intention not to respect its serious duties and its sacred laws. Now, marriage, St. Liguori tells us, has two essential and intrinsic ends, which are: the reciprocal right over themselves which the spouses give to each other, and the indissolubility of the bond that unites them. Whoever, then, on getting married, would exclude positively both these ends, would not only sin grievously, but also render his marriage invalid. This is the common teaching of theologians.†

"The first motive that ought to actuate persons entering the married state is, therefore, the bond of a society in conformity with natural

---

* Suar., *De statu perf.*, lib. 1, c. ix, n. 28.
† St. Lig., *Theol. Mor.*, lib. 6, tr. 6, n. 882.

inclinations, which gives to each of the contracting parties the hope of mutual help in bearing the hardships of life, and the infirmities of old age." *

Marriage has, furthermore, two intrinsic, but accidental ends, continues St. Liguori, which are: children, and protection against sin. These two ends, to be good and praiseworthy, must be referred to God, if not actually, at least virtually and habitually.†

This teaching of St. Liguori is, likewise, that of the catechism of the Council of Trent, which develops it thus: The second motive (that should actuate people in getting married) is the desire to have children; less, to leave heirs for their wealth and fortunes, than to bring them up in the practice of the Christian religion. This was the special object of the patriarchs; hence, the angel, when teaching Tobias how to repel the attacks of the Evil Spirit, said to him: "Hear me, and I will show thee who they are, over whom the devil can prevail. For they who in such manner receive matrimony as to shut out God from themselves and from their mind, and to give themselves to their lust . . . over them the devil hath power." (Chap. vi, 16, 17). And he added: "Thou shalt take the virgin with the fear of the Lord, moved rather for love of children." (Ibid. 22.) The third motive that may be had, has been

---

* *Catech. Conc. Trid. de matrim.*, n. 15.
† St. Lig., *Theol. Mor.*, lib. 6, tr. 6, n. 882.

added to the others since the fall of our first parents. He who has experience of his weakness, and does not wish always to struggle against his temptations, may have recourse to marriage as a safeguard against sin.

These are the virtuous ends, some one of which is to be willed by him who seeks to contract marriage religiously and piously, as children of saints ought to do.

If, to these reasons, others are superadded, leading men to marry, or to prefer one spouse to another,—for instance, to have an heir, wealth, beauty, birth, harmony of character,—they cannot be condemned, since they are not at variance with the holiness of marriage. The Scripture addresses no reproach to Jacob for preferring Rachel to Lia on account of her beauty.* Yet, as St. Liguori remarks, it would be disorderly to enter marriage chiefly for ends accidental and extrinsic to that state, and not good in themselves. Hence, it would not be right to marry from vainglory, from avarice, or any view of that kind.†

Nowadays, unhappily, marriages are too often inspired, above all, by similar motives; virtue is not taken into account, and perishable interests alone guide the calculations of a prudence reprobated alike by reason and by faith! Philip, Prefect of Egypt, pressed Saint Eugenia, his

---

* *Catech. Conc. Trid. de matrim.*, n. 15.
† St. Lig., *Theol. Mor.*, lib. 6, tr. 6, n. 883.

daughter, to give her hand to the son of a consul named Aquilius, whose nobility he extolled. Eugenia was, at that time, only fifteen, and she answered: "In a husband one must consider virtue, and not birth; for he, and not his parents, is accepted in marriage." It is related that a father one day asked Themistocles, whether it were better to give one's daughter in marriage to a poor man with virtue, or to a rich man without virtue. "Were I in your place," replied Themistocles, "I would prefer a man with money to money without a man."* Christians, to-day, do not always rise to the same heights as pagan wisdom.

How long, O children of men! will you love vanity, and seek after lying? What blindness prompts you to pursue what flatters your self-love or your avarice, rather than what would make you happy? Are you, then, ignorant that virtue alone holds the promises of the life that now is, and of the life to come? It constitutes the bliss of marriage, and it is it that married persons should seek before all things. "A virtuous woman rejoiceth her husband, and shall fulfil the years of his life in peace. A good wife is a good portion: she shall be given, in the portion of them that fear God, to man for his good deeds." (Ecclus. xxvi, 2, 3.) And we can subjoin, that a young woman may look forward

---

* Valer. Max. *in auri fodina, voc. conjugium.*

to a happy future only in so far forth as she chooses for her husband one who is a Christian, devoted to the faith of the Church, and to the practice of the duties which she prescribes.

Tertullian has drawn a picture of the sufferings of Christian women who, in his day, married unbelieving husbands. His words have a literal application to many who now marry the indifferent Christians in whom our age abounds: " Who can doubt that faith daily grows dim in the company of an unbeliever? How can the wife keep God's law who has constantly at her side a companion of devils? If there is question of going to the assemblies of the faithful, her husband seeks to draw her to profane places. When there should be fast, he commands a feast for the same day. Will that husband allow his wife to go around visiting the huts of the poor? Can you, O woman! hide from him the sign of the cross which you make on your bed and on yourself? Can you, at night, without his notice, rise for prayer? Will he not consider your pious practices as sheer superstitions? What will he say to you? Will he speak of or read the Scriptures with you? Where, then, will you find solace for your soul? How bless the Lord with him, since there is no bond of union between you?" *

---

* Tertull., *Ad uxor.*, lib. 2, c. ii, etc. Ed. Migne.

CHAPTER V.

CHIEF CASES IN WHICH MARRIAGE IS UNLAWFUL OR INVALID.

IN the first place, as St. Liguori teaches, although it is certain that marriages contracted by young persons without the consent of their parents are valid,* "still young persons should be taught so far to honor their parents, or those holding their place, as not to get married without warning them, much less against their will." These words are taken from the catechism of the Council of Trent, and it adds: "It is to be remarked that in the Old Law children were given and settled in marriage by their parents."†

It would be a grievous sin to marry after having taken a vow of chastity, a vow to enter religion, not to marry, or a vow to receive holy orders. For good reasons, these vows can be changed. Dispensation from the vow of perpetual chastity, or to enter a religious order, is reserved to the pope. The order of subdeaconship, and the profession of religious whose vows are considered solemn by the Holy See, render subsequent

---
* *Theol. Mor.*, lib. 6, tr. 6, n. 849.   † *De matrim.*, n. 37.

marriage not only unlawful, but null and void, according to the express teaching of the Council of Trent.* Valid betrothment that has not been duly annulled, carries with it an obligation to marry the affianced. It would be a sin against justice to marry another person, unless some suitable cause warrants the breaking-off of the previous engagement. It is certain, says St. Liguori, that an affianced person, who vows to enter religion, does a lawful act. He should keep his vow, and, if he really desires to become a religious, he is not bound by his engagement to marry, unless he were not to persevere in religion. A vow of chastity, whether preceding, or following upon, an engagement to marry, annuls the engagement.†

A marriage contracted by a baptized Christian and an unbeliever, who is not baptized, is invalid, unless a dispensation be obtained from the Church previous to the marriage. But, if a Catholic, without dispensation, marries a heretic, the contract is valid, though grievously illicit. Dispensation for a marriage of this kind is granted only on the condition that all the children shall be brought up in the Catholic religion. The illustrious Pope Benedict XIV says that the Church has always detested such marriages; and he earnestly exhorts pastors to use all their efforts efficaciously to hinder them, and make them be

---

* Sess. 24, can. 9.   † St. Lig., *Theol. Mor.*, lib. 6, tr. 6, n. 873.

looked upon with fear by Catholics, for whom they may prove a source of spiritual ruin.*

A Protestant gentleman, as distinguished for the nobility of his blood as for the graces of his person, asked for the hand of Jane Frances Frémiot, who afterward became the famous Baroness de Chantal, and foundress of the Visitation Nuns. In vain did the parents of the young girl insist that the believing wife would convert the unbelieving husband: they were unable to obtain her consent to such an alliance. One day, when urged more than usual, "I would rather choose," said she, "a perpetual prison for my lodging than the house of a Huguenot; and I would prefer a thousand deaths, one after the other, to seeing myself bound by marriage to an enemy of the Church." At first, these words caused astonishment, for the young man concealed his true sentiments, and appeared to be a Catholic; but he threw off the mask as soon as he saw that there was no hope for him to win the hand of Jane Frances Frémiot.†

But we have said enough on this subject. Our purpose is not to furnish a complete treatise on the impediments to matrimony of divine or ecclesiastical origin. The faithful ought to be acquainted with them, and to respect them everywhere.

Let us, then, bring this subject to a close in the

---

* St. Lig., ibid., n. 1044.   † Her Life, by the Abbé Bougand.

words of St. John Chrysostom: "Do not dishonor marriage by diabolical feasts. If you banish from them unbecoming, effeminate singing, dances, improper conversation, the pomps of Satan, noise, boisterous laughter, intemperance, with all that is unbecoming in Christians, Christ will be present at the wedding. But it is Satan who presides at those weddings at which voluptuous and disgraceful dancing is indulged in; and, from all the expenses incurred on such occasions, great harm results, and no profit is derived."*

ARTICLE II.

The Unmarried State.

Suarez says: "It is clear that married persons are in the common condition of the Christian life. For, in reference to the spiritual life, marriage, of itself, adds nothing to the general state of the faithful; and it calls for no further perfection than what is essential to charity, and what the profession of the Christian religion demands. Indeed, among married persons, there may be a high degree of holiness and good works; yet their state does not make that high degree imperative, nor does it offer any special assistance for its attainment. It is, therefore, called an imperfect state; not that it debars from perfection, but

---

* *Homil. in propter fornicationem unusquisque*, etc. Ed. Migne, vol. 3, col. 210, 211.

because, in itself, it does not impel to perfection." *
"If, in the Church of Christ, it receives from its character, as sacrament, a certain measure of perfection, all it gains from that dignity is greater stability and more abundant grace to surmount with generosity the difficulties and dangers that surround it." † The learned theologian adds: "The faithful, not engaged in the married state, or who have entered no perfect state, are not to be shut out from the general state of the Christian life. Nor among them are to be ranked those who, in the world, live in celibacy, virginity, or widowhood." We shall consider, one after the other, these different conditions of Christian life.

Paragraph 1.—*Celibacy.*

With regard to celibacy, we must, in imitation of Suarez, begin by speaking on the errors of heretics. Some heretics said marriage was forbidden, and they consequently condemned it altogether. As a necessary result of this doctrine, they held celibacy to be obligatory. ‡ Helvidius and Jovinian, though they did not go the length of censuring celibacy, taught, however, that it was no better than marriage. Protestants revived this old heresy, which St. Jerome had crushed; and they taught that to observe celibacy, or virginity, is a matter of no consequence, and, therefore, it

---

* Suar., lib. 1, c. ii, n. 13.   † Ibid., n. 14.
‡ Ibid., *De voto cast.*, lib. 9, c. i, n. 1.

is superstitious to vow it to God.* With still greater boldness than the Protestants, the freethinkers of more modern times are not ashamed to assert that celibacy is impossible and contrary to nature. These errors, which publish the shame of those who profess them, have invaded the minds of men calling themselves Catholics, while reserving for themselves the right to think as heretics and impious men. As to us, we lay down, in conformity with the doctors of the Church, the following propositions: Firstly, even perpetual celibacy is possible. Secondly, it is not obligatory, but only a counsel. Thirdly, it is a happier state than that of marriage. Fourthly, it is also a more perfect state. Fifthly, it is praiseworthy to vow it. Sixthly, persons may be advised to practise it. Seventhly, no one can, without just cause, be prevented from embracing it.

What we have to say on celibacy is, to a certain degree, applicable to virginity and widowhood, of which we shall say a few words farther on. Before, however, entering on this subject, we have to observe that, in treating of marriage, we dealt with it as it is in itself, and not as it is among those who profane it. We shall speak of celibacy in the same way, for we are comparing states, and not persons. We have said nothing of faithless or guilty spouses; neither shall we say anything of those who, free from the bands of wedlock,

---

* Suarez, ibid., n. 2.

or living a single life, do not, withal, observe perfect chastity. Let it suffice here to warn that nothing stained shall enter heaven, and that, if persons refrain from marriage, which is allowable, they should keep still farther away from what is forbidden. The commandments of God condemn even guilty thoughts and desires.

CHAPTER I.

CELIBACY IS POSSIBLE.

It is quite true, says Suarez, that, without a gift from God, that is, without the help of his grace, we cannot fully observe perpetual chastity, nor even temporary chastity, for a long time. But it is also equally true that, with the assistance of divine grace, which never fails him, a man has it in his power to obtain this gift from God by prayer and other good works. This assistance is clearly promised in Scripture; besides, it is evident from experience that many souls receive this favor through the means which we have pointed out, and keep spotless the chastity which they have vowed. This shows that the impossibility asserted by heretics means nothing more than their own evil inclinations and perversity of will. "You cannot," says Tertullian, "because you will not." *

From the words of our Lord, " He that can take, let him take " (Matt. xix, 12) the counsel of celibacy, Calvin, one of the chiefs of Protestantism, inferred that men are dissuaded from, rather than invited to, the practice of celibacy.† But,

---

* Suar., *De voto cast.*, lib. 9, c. i, n. 24.   † Ibid., n. 21.

as St. Thomas and St. Jerome remark, "these words are the voice of Jesus Christ exhorting his soldiers, and rousing them to merit the rewards of chastity. It is as though he were to say: Let him who can combat, enter the arena; let him bear off the victory and triumph."* "Now," concludes Suarez, "Christ would not incite men to what is impossible." † Cornelius à Lapide is still more explicit. "The faithful," he says, "can, by the grace of Christ, practise virginity, or celibacy,—an effort that is beyond the power of unbelievers." All do not take this word, namely, the counsel of chastity; all do not accept or embrace it: they alone do it on whom God has bestowed the great gift of continence. Here we must keep in mind that, though all the faithful have not the gift of continence, so as to actually practise chastity; as all the just have not the gift of perseverance, so as to actually persevere in justice,—however, since all the just have the gift of perseverance so as to be able to continue in justice if they wish it, in like manner, all the faithful possess the gift of continence to the extent of being able to observe chastity in case they wish; that is to say, if they frequently beg of God strength and grace to practise that virtue, and if they coöperate with God's grace, by watching over their senses, shunning idleness, having recourse to bodily mortification, and the

---

* S. Th., opusc. 18, c. viii.   † Suar., ibid., n. 25.

other means of preserving chastity. This is the teaching of St. Chrysostom, Origen, Theophylact, Euthymius, St. Jerome, St. Augustine, St. Ambrose and others. It follows, besides, from the very words of the Gospel. Christ therein advises every Christian to keep chastity. But that alone can be counselled which is under the control of free-will, and within the power of man, aided by grace,—a grace which God always holds in readiness, and offers to every one that asks him for it. It is not so with the gift of prophecy or miracles. God does not prepare these for, nor offer them to, all. They are for a chosen few only, whom he destines for the general good of the Church.*

The learned commentator, in another place, declares it to be the common opinion of the fathers of the Church that celibacy is in our power if we beg it of God, and if, with heroic courage, we endeavor to put it in practice. Every man can, if he wishes, live in that state, however inclined he may be to sin through nature or habit. St. Paul intimates the same plainly enough, when he exhorts all to virginity; and we know that nothing is counselled or ordained save what we can do by the grace of God.† This doctrine should console weak and tempted souls.

---

* Corn. à Lapide in Matt. 19.
† Comment. in cap. vii, 1 ad Cor., ver. 25.

St. Augustine writes in his Confessions: "These trifles of trifles, these vanities of vanities, pulled me by the garment of my flesh, and whispered to me: 'Do you send us away? What! Shall we never more abide with you? And how now, shall this and that be no longer granted you—and forever?' On the side to which I turned, and where I feared to pass, stood Continence, in chaste majesty, inviting me no longer with the smile of the courtesan, but with the purest caresses, to draw near her without fear; she stretched out her holy arms to receive and embrace me, and pointed with her hand to countless bright examples—to children, tender maidens, young men above number, persons of every age, venerable widows and virgins with the snows of years on their brows. And the lovely form seemed to say to me with a sweet and cheering voice of irony: 'What! You cannot do what these children and these weak women have achieved? Is it, then, of themselves, and not in the Lord God, that such a life has been possible for them? O, cast yourself boldly on him, have no fear; he will not withdraw, nor allow you to fall.'"* St. Augustine followed the advice of Chastity, and was victorious in this contest of the soul.

From what we have just said, it is manifest that, even in the midst of the world, celibacy is not

---

* *Conf.*, lib. 8, c. xi.

impossible; and, although religious houses offer a secure shelter to chastity, it would be against the experience of all ages, since Christianity came into the world, to say that celibacy cannot be thought of save in a convent. It is well known that in Western Europe many Christian virgins lived in their families. Indeed, in every age and country, numerous virgins have shone out in the world in all the splendor of purity and self-immolation. Besides, the Church imposes celibacy on all her ministers, not excepting even those who live in the world.

CHAPTER II.

IS CELIBACY PERMITTED, OR IS IT A PRECEPT OR A COUNSEL.

"It is lawful to keep perpetual virginity and continence. This assertion is of faith," says Suarez. "The reason of it is, that there is no precept binding all men, or every one of them, to spend even a part of their life in marriage."* Furthermore, we must remember, according to St. Thomas, that man possesses three sorts of goods, namely: goods external to himself,—such as wealth,—goods of the body, and goods of the soul. External, or goods opportune, are inferior to those of the body; and the goods of the body themselves are beneath those of the soul. In the goods of the soul, those having reference to active life are of less importance than what appertains to contemplative life. It is, therefore, a dictate of right reason that we should use riches in so far as they subserve the body; and the goods of the body, in so far as they are beneficial to the soul. If, then, we forego the possession of certain things that are lawful in themselves, with a view to preserve our health, or give ourselves

---

* *De voto cast.*, lib. 9, c. i, nn. 3, 4.

up to the contemplation of truth, we incur no guilt, and only follow the teachings of reason. The same holds with respect to the pleasures of the body. It is reasonable to abstain from them for the purpose of devoting one's self to the study of truth. Now, this is just what virginity or celibacy does. Therefore, these two modes of living are innocent and praiseworthy.*

However, where a person has taken no vow, celibacy is not obligatory, as we proved when we showed that marriage is a holy and lawful state. St. Paul teaches this very plainly where he says (1 Cor. vii, 25): "Now, concerning virgins, I have no commandment of the Lord;" that is, no obligation for them to lead a life of celibacy. "The Lord, who is indulgent, and who knows that the spirit is quick and the flesh weak, did not wish to force virginity on us, but has left it," says St. Chrysostom, "to our own free choice. He passes no sentence of condemnation upon such as do not feel in themselves courage enough to embrace that state, and yet he has opened to others a noble and glorious career."† "Had the Lord made virginity imperative, he would have seemed to condemn marriage, and deprive men of the means to keep up their race. He would, likewise, have rendered virgins impossible: for, cut away the root, and where will you gather fruit? Do not, therefore, be surprised that, in the

---

* St. Th., 2, 2, q. 152, a. 2. † St. Chrysost., *De virginitate*, c. ii.

midst of the revolts of the flesh and the fires of concupiscence, God has contented himself with teaching us, but has not forced on us the life of heavenly spirits."*

But does not celibacy fall within the counsels? Not only is it allowed, says Suarez, but it is better to keep virginity; and for this reason it is counselled, though not commanded, in the Gospel law. This assertion is of faith, because it is expressly affirmed and proved by St. Paul when he says: "Concerning virgins, I have no command of the Lord, but I give counsel" (1 Cor. vii, 25)—to live in virginity, as à Lapide explains it. This learned commentator remarks that the counsel is given to all—*omnibus consuli*.† The Apostle of the Gentiles had indeed previously said: "I would that all men were even as myself" (1 Cor. vii, 7); that is, led a life of celibacy. We have already cited this passage from the catechism of the Council of Trent: "Virginity is sovereignly recommended in Scripture and counselled to every one, because it is more profitable, and fuller of holiness and perfection, than the marriage state."‡ Yet Suarez remarks that virginity would not be a counsel for one whom some very important public good, or a similar reason, would oblige to marry.§ But this is an exceptional case. Here is the rule laid down by

---

* St. Hieron. adv. Jovin., lib. 1, 12. † In 1 Cor. vii, 25.
‡ *De matrim.*, n. 1. § *De statu perf.*, lib. 1, c. vii, n. 7.

the Council of Trent: "If any saith that the marriage state is placed above the state of virginity or of celibacy, and that it is not better and more blessed to remain in virginity or in celibacy than to be united in matrimony,—let him be anathema."[*] Such is the faith of the Church; and it ought to be the rule of the thoughts, sentiments, and words of every Catholic. To assert that marriage is to be preferred before celibacy, that it is as good and as blessed as celibacy, would be to incur the Tridentine anathema. But we must throw more light on this truth, and speak briefly on the advantages and excellence of a life spent in the practice of perfect chastity.

---

[*] Sess. 24, can. 10. (Waterworth's trans.)

CHAPTER III.

CELIBACY IS A HAPPIER STATE THAN MARRIAGE.

To prefer virginity is not, as St. Jerome observes, a depreciation of marriage.* Silver does not cease to be silver, because gold is more precious. It is no injury to a tree to have its fruits preferred to its leaves or roots. As a tree bears fruit, so marriage bears celibacy ;† and the higher our esteem for celibacy, the more should we make of marriage which gives birth to virgins.‡ We need not fear, then, to enumerate, with the holy fathers and doctors of the Church, the privileges and advantages of perfect chastity. Those that marry shall have tribulation of the flesh, says St. Paul. "But I would have you to be without solicitude. He that is without a wife is solicitous for the things that belong to the Lord, how he may please God. But he that is with a wife is solicitous for the things of the world, how he may please his wife; and he is divided. And the unmarried woman and the virgin thinketh on the things of the Lord, that she may be holy both in body and in spirit. But

---

* Epist. 22 ad Eustoch., 19. Ed. Migne.
† Contra Jovin., lib. I, 1.
‡ Ad Eustoch. 20. Ed. Migne., epist. 19.

she that is married thinketh on the things of the world, how she may please her husband." (1 Cor. vii.) In commenting on these ends, the fathers and commentators speak, at great length, on the difficulties of married life. St. Jerome, writing to Eustochium, speaks to her of the sufferings of the wife, the annoying cries of children, and of widowhood that often soon follows upon marriage.*

SS. Basil and Chrysostom speak still more openly. The latter compares the two spouses to a pair of runaway slaves tightly bound by a single chain. They can take only a few steps, because the stirring of one hinders and inconveniences the other.† The practice of virtue in the married state is all the more troublesome, that the care of a wife and anxiety about children are a bar to the soul, and draw it back to the preoccupation of earth. ‡ It is therefore true to say that, if man finds in woman some help for a weak and slender form of virtue, she becomes an obstacle for him as soon as he wishes to walk in the path of perfection.§ When walking along a road that is narrow and hedged with thorns, we can shun the difficulties of the road only by exposing ourselves to be lacerated by the thorns; so, in the married life, one inconvenience avoided exposes us to incur a still greater.‖

---

* Epist. 22, ad Eustoch.
† St. Hieron. ad Eustoch., epist. 22, n. 15.
‡ St. Chrysost., *De virginitate*, c. xli.
§ Ibid. c. xliv.   ‖ Ibid., c. xlvi, 52.

St. Liguori, addressing virgins, says to them, with all the authority of his knowledge and experience: "Poor mothers of families meet with many bars to holiness; and the more shining their rank in the world, the more numerous these obstacles become. . . . What leisure, what help, what recollection, can a married woman find to devote herself constantly to God?" . . . Where can she get much time for prayer, since often she has no time for the duties of her household? Her husband wishes to be waited on, and he complains. Servants disturb the peace of the family by their talk and their quarrels. The children, if young, cry, scream, and are forever calling for something; when they are grown up, they are an endless cause of anxiety and trouble, either on account of the bad company which they keep, or on account of the diseases to which they are so liable. How hard to pray or be recollected amid such turmoil and anguish!

"It is true that the married woman could merit a great deal from the privation of the happiness of prayer, were she patiently to bear with her thraldom. She could merit; but in the midst of such noise, without prayer or sacraments, it is almost hopeless to expect such resignation. Would to heaven that married women were open to no other blame than that of being hindered in their desire for prayer! They must look to their rank; they must pay their servants; they must converse, at least during visits, with every class of persons; and in their own houses they must receive the relatives, the connections, and the friends of their husbands. How many occasions are there not in all this for losing God! Young girls do not know all the danger to which they expose themselves in marrying, but women already married have a full knowledge of them."* In quoting these words of the illustrious and holy bishop, we have somewhat toned them down, as any one can see for himself by reference to the work from which we have taken this passage.

It would be superfluous to go into greater lengths on this subject. Protestants themselves have acknowledged the superiority of celibacy, in that it frees men efficaciously from the trammels and annoyances of this life. Some of them went so far as to assert that it makes man fitter for the worship of God and the practice of religion.† Indeed, this point is clear from the authorities that we have adduced, as well as from experience. How many souls altogether devoted to God and good works before marriage, almost directly after it, not only gave up pious practices, but even the ordinary duties of a Christian life! Family cares made them lose sight of the claims of their eternal interests. In

---

* St. Lig., "The Religious Sanctified." (First chapter.)
† Corn. à Lapide in 1 Cor. vii, 34.

other cases, piety and devotedness to noble works seek refuge in those hearts which perfect chastity throws open to them.

Were any one to object that the hindrances to virtue of married persons render their state more meritorious than celibacy, we would say no, borrowing the thought of St. Chrysostom; for they raised up these barriers for themselves, while it was in their power to avoid them. With the same father, we would ask what merit there can be in freely embracing a state in which salvation is more difficult, when something far better could be done. Merit and virtue, asserts the Angelical, consist far more in the good which is their object, than in the difficulties which they present.* Hence, then, what is most difficult is not therefore the most meritorious. That which presents more difficulties must also be accompanied by greater good, in order to be of higher merit.†

---

* *De virginitate*, n. 45. † 2, 2, q. 27, a. 8, ad. 3.

CHAPTER IV.

IS CELIBACY BETTER THAN MARRIAGE.

Let us first note with Suarez that persons free from the bonds of wedlock are fitter for the state of perfection than those who are married.* Perfect chastity, says the same great theologian, is not only praiseworthy in that it makes man free and fitter for spiritual things, but also because it is in itself more lovely, better, more honorable, and, at the same time, richer in merits.† In itself chastity unites the heart to God, and withdraws, as far as possible, man from animal life, to raise him to a spiritual existence. For this reason the fathers liken virginity to the state and perfection of angels, because it, in a certain measure, makes men imitate angelic life, according to the words of the Saviour: "In the resurrection they shall neither marry nor be married; but shall be as the angels of God in heaven." (Matt. xxii, 30.) "What is to be consummated by the glory of the resurrection of our bodies is here undertaken by holy men through the perfection of their chastity. Hence, St. Cyril of Jerusalem teaches that this

---

* *De statu perfect.*, lib. I, c. ii.   † *De voto cast.*, c. i, n. 12.

perfect chastity is above man, and is the crown of the angels."*

Finally, as by celibacy man acquires greater merit, so it consequently gives him a right to a higher reward in heaven. Indeed, an ancient author, supposed to be St. Athanasius, writing to a young person, broke forth into these exclamations: "O perfect chastity, friend of God, and praised of saints! O continence, hated of many, but dearly valued and loved of those who are able to understand thee! thou overthrowest death and Satan, and art the dower of immortal spirits. O continence, joy of prophets, glory of apostles, life of angels, and crown of saints! blessed are they who possess thee! In them the pains of a moment borne for thy sake will bring thee abundant joys."† From what has just been said, it is easy to infer, and very important to understand, how proper it was for the Church not to admit her ministers to holy orders before making them promise continence, or perpetual celibacy. Suarez observes that reason and natural right sufficiently show the wisdom of this action of the Church; and he adds: "In the Old Law, it is true, God did not prescribe perfect chastity to his priests: the sacrifices of mere animals which they had to offer up did not require such purity. Yet they were held to continence during the

---

* *De voto cast.*, c. i, n. 14.
† *Inter op. St. Athan.*, *De virginitate*. Ed. Migne, tom. 4, col. 279.

time of their functions in the temple. Thereby God showed how becoming it is that his ministers should altogether abstain from even the awful pleasures of the senses."* Indeed, ecclesiastical celibacy is entirely in keeping with the precepts and counsels of the Gospel; for our Lord recommended chastity to all, and taught the practice of it, especially, to his apostles. St. Paul advises the faithful leading the married life to refrain for a time by mutual consent, in order to give themselves up to prayer. It is therefore, with just reason, far more becoming that the ministers of the Church, who from duty must often pray and perform their sacred functions, should be free from the bonds of matrimony.†

"And, in truth, the duties of a minister of God, particularly of a pastor, are not limited to prayer and the altar. He is bound to confer sacraments, especially penance, to instruct by word and example, and to assist the sick. He is the father of the poor, of the widow, of the orphan, and of the forlorn child. His flock is his family; he is the distributor of alms, the resource of all the unfortunate. This multitude of painful and harassing functions is incompatible with the cares, perplexities, and vexations of the marriage state. A married priest would be at a loss to gain for himself the respect and confidence required for the success of his ministry.‡

---

* *De voto cast.*, lib. o, c. xiii, nn. 13, 14. † Ibid., n. 15.
‡ Bergier, "*Dictionnaire de Theol.*," verbo *Célibat.*

Hence the practice of celibacy by the clergy was in honor from the beginning of Christianity, as Suarez proves at great length;* and the Council of Trent consecrated its obligation by hurling an anathema against those who would dare to say that clerics constituted in sacred orders are able to contract marriage, and that, being contracted, it is valid; and that all who do not feel that they have the gift of chastity, even though they have made a vow thereof, may contract marriage, seeing that God refuses not that gift to those who ask for it rightly; neither does he suffer us to be tempted above that which we are able.† (1 Cor. x, 13.) But it is time to return to our subject.

---

* *De voto cast.*, lib. 9, c. xiv.   † Sess. 24, can. 9.

CHAPTER V.

THE VOW OF CHASTITY.

To live a life of celibacy or virginity, without having vowed it, is a counsel; and it is another counsel, says Suarez, to vow it.* It is good, and even very good, to consecrate to God by vow our perpetual chastity. This assertion is of faith, if we view the vow in itself and in its matter, and leave aside accidental circumstances.† It may be proved from the fathers and councils. Their testimonies are so numerous and clear, that even heretics cannot deny them; there is therefore no need to tarry with them. But we cannot omit confirming this truth by some very striking examples. The first and noblest that we have in the law of grace is that given by the ever Blessed Virgin Mary, who made a vow of chastity; and I have proved elsewhere that her illustrious spouse, St. Joseph, did the same. It is likely, but not certain, that our Lord had a similar vow. However, it is beyond all doubt that Jesus Christ was the pattern most perfect of virginity vowed to God; either because he consecrated his

---

* *De statu perf.*, lib. 1, c. viii, n. 3.
† *De voto cast.*, lib. 9, c. i, n. 16.

virginity, not by a vow only, but by the divinity itself (he chose virginity as a state absolutely suited to his adorable person, and from the instant of his conception he determined immovably to keep it); or because the vow of the Blessed Virgin has its root in Jesus Christ, was inspired and taken in view of that divine Saviour, and by way of preparation for his coming.* These glorious examples have had many imitators in the course of ages, as we shall mention later on.

But reason itself affords us another proof of the statement. A matter good, and better than its opposite, can be the subject of a vow. Now, perfect chastity, as we have seen, is good and better than the state which is incompatible with it: hence, it can be the object of a vow. Therefore the vow of chastity is excellent; and to keep it by vow is better than to keep it without vow.† And indeed St. Thomas proves abundantly that it is preferable to do good and vow to do so, than to do the same good without any vow.‡ Greater generosity is displayed in giving away the tree with its fruit, than in making a present of the fruit only.

A vow of perfect chastity binds a person to abstain from every exterior, and even interior, act contrary to it, such as an impure thought or desire; insomuch that were one, under this vow,

---

* Suar., *De voto cast.*, lib. 9, c. i, n. 19. † Ibid., n. 21.
‡ St. Th., opusc. 18, c. xii.

deliberately to consent, even interiorly, to any act of the kind, he would commit a double mortal sin—one against the sixth commandment of God, and another against religion, by violating his vow.* When that person goes to confession, he or she must not only tell the sin committed, but make known, besides, the vow of chastity which they have taken.

In the next place, a vow of chastity binds one not to enter the marriage state. This double obligation lasts for life in the case of a vow of perpetual chastity. Where the vow is intended only for a limited time, the obligation remains until the end of the time for which it was made. When a person simply and absolutely vows chastity, he is to be considered as having contracted the twofold obligation that we have spoken of, namely: to abstain from every act, exterior and interior, of impurity, and not to marry. According to Suarez, the case is the same when virginity is vowed without any restriction.† Yet, as the binding force of a vow is only what the one taking the vow wishes to impose on himself, it may happen that a person taking the vow of perpetual chastity intends to promise God only certain acts of that virtue. Therefore, virginity can be vowed with the express purpose of not vowing perfect chastity; and this partial vow of virginity obliges only not

---

* Suar., *De voto cast.*, lib. 9, c. ii, n. 2.   † Ibid., c. iii, n. 15.

to marry, or not to do any external act contrary to virginity. A person can also take the vow not to marry; in which case one does not sin against his vow, unless he actually marries, or desires to do so. A perpetual and absolute vow of perfect chastity is reserved to the Holy See; that is to say, ordinarily speaking, the Sovereign Pontiff alone can dispense from it.

After what we have said, the inference is plain that what heightens the merit of generous souls, what strengthens them in their resolves and links them more closely to God, is, for weak, inconstant, and unfaithful souls, an occasion of grievous sin. Therefore, says St. Clement, no one should make to God rash and thoughtless promises. We should be prudent in our actions, for it is better never to bind one's self by vow than not to fulfil the obligation when it has been contracted.* It is, then, important not to vow chastity before taking the advice of a prudent, learned, and virtuous confessor. The directors of souls should not lose sight of the wise advice given by St. Liguori: "Do not allow young women to take a vow of perpetual chastity unless they are known to be solidly virtuous, instructed in the rules of the spiritual life, and accustomed to prayer. In the beginning, they can be allowed to take the vow only from one feast to another."†

---

* *Lib. Const. Apost.*, cap. i, apud Suar., ibid., c. i, n. 18.
† *Praxis confess.*, n. 93.

However, if it is inconsiderate to allow the vow of chastity to be taken without discretion, would it not be far more grievous to make it a maxim and an invariable rule to stifle and repress always the holy desire to consecrate one's self to God which grace begets in Christian souls?

What has been said should teach persons who have vowed their chastity to God, how much they ought to be in dread of sins which their sacred engagements render still more terrible. "He that thinketh himself to stand, let him take heed lest he fall." (1 Cor. 10, 12.) Therefore, let them guard against occasions, and take means to preserve their purity of soul and body. They should be faithful in frequenting the sacraments, and persevere in prayer.

CHAPTER VI.

IS IT LAWFUL TO EXHORT OTHERS TO THE PRACTICE OF PERFECT CHASTITY OR CELIBACY.

WE can exhort others to what is possible, permitted, and better. Now, with the exception of a few accidental cases, celibacy, which is always possible, is allowed, and is better. Hence, as a general rule, and saving the exceptions, celibacy can be advised. Our Lord did not hesitate to do it. "For fear," says St. Thomas, "that some would not tend, according to their graces, to win the gift of perfect chastity, the Lord gives a general exhortation to it; first, by setting before our eyes the example of those who practise continence: 'There are eunuchs,' etc.; and next, by holding out to us the reward of chastity—'for the kingdom of heaven.' (Matt. xix, 12.) Lastly, he exhorts to it, when he says: 'He that can take, let him take it' (ibid.),—words which are, according to St. Jerome, the voice of Jesus Christ cheering his soldiers and challenging them to merit the palm of chastity. It is as though he were to say: Let him who can combat, enter the lists; let him conquer and triumph."*

In imitation of his Master, St. Paul does not hesitate to say to the faithful: "I would wish that all were like myself;" and he portrays for the Corinthians the excellence and profit of virginity.† It was in consequence of the exhortations of this great apostle that St. Thecla embraced virginity; and he himself was put to death by Nero because he wrested from the passions of the tyrant young Christian maidens, whom he consecrated to God, as Cornelius à Lapide relates.‡ St. Matthew, continues the distinguished commentator, persuaded St. Iphigenia, daughter of the King of Ethiopia, to vow her virginity to God.

St. Clement, a relative of the Emperor Domitian, led a life of perpetual virginity. He has left admirable eulogies of that virtue, and taught it to others, as every one can see by reading his letters. His example and advice induced the emperor's niece, Flavia Domitilla, the affianced of Aurelian, to practise faithfully before God the chastity she had vowed to him. The holy pontiff did not hesitate to give her the virgin's veil, though he thereby exposed himself and the Christians to the fury of Domitian. What man of mere worldly prudence, says à Lapide, would

---

* St. Th., opusc. 18, c. viii. † 1 Cor. vii, 7.
‡ In Apoc. xiv, 4, et 1 Cor. vii, 34.

not have looked upon such conduct as unwise? But St. Clement, prudent after the manner of God, knew that virginity is of such worth in the eyes of heaven, that it may be purchased even at the cost of martyrdom. He was aware that God watches over his own, and that it is heroism not to give way before threats of death, particularly where there is question of preserving the treasure of virginity.* Those who have read the fathers and doctors of the Church, and chiefly SS. Athanasius, Chrysostom, Basil, Ambrose, Jerome, Augustine, and Bernard, have not to be taught how much these illustrious men labored to make celibacy and virginity known and loved by mankind. These great sons of holy Church spread their wings in eagle flight, and rose to the noblest heights of eloquence, when descanting on this inspiring theme. St. Ambrose ranks among the foremost, and may justly be called the Doctor of perfect chastity. It was the favorite subject of his sermons. Certain mothers, who, while professing Christianity, retained a coloring of paganism, forbade their daughters to go to hear the eloquent bishop. Matters went so far, that he was even accused of disturbing families, endangering the empire, and drying up human life in its very source.†

But Ambrose defended himself in this way:

---

* In Apoc. 14, et in Isa. lxvi, 5.
† See his beautiful Life by the Abbé Baunard.

"They say that I preach perfect chastity and counsel it to many. Would to God that facts could convict me of doing what is laid to my charge! I would be in no fear of the hatred of my assailants, if I saw my words producing any fruit. Shall not those who take a man for their husband be allowed to give the preference to God? Why do to me what is done to no one else, and cast up to me, as a disgrace, that which is the glory of other priests, namely: to scatter in souls the seed of virtue, and entice them to a life of virginity?"* St. Augustine, who was trained in the school of Ambrose, wished such as had tasted the pure joys of chastity to share them with others. He wrote to the widow Juliana and to the virgin Demetrias: "By the pattern of your lives, and by your words of exhortation, draw all that you can to your career"—the practice of continence.† These lessons did not remain without echo. A corrupted society was dotted with the glowing flowers of chastity; and in an atmosphere, thick with the abominations of paganism, the fairest of virtues breathed its perfume.

In the fourth century, according to the testimony of St. Ambrose himself, more virgins gave themselves to God in Africa and the East, than all the men he knew of in Italy.

On one occasion the illustrious bishop consecrated to God as many as eight hundred, and

---

* *De virginitate*, c. v, nn. 25, 26.   † *De bono viduitatis*, c. xxviii.

the ceremony lasted three days.* We read, in the history of the Church, that in the same century there were in Oxyrinchus, a town of Lower Thebais, as many as twenty thousand virgins.† In the middle ages, writes Father Ventura, every family deemed itself honored and happy to give a spouse to Christ. For families having many daughters, it was looked upon as a disgrace and a misfortune not to have one in the holy state of virginity. Fathers and mothers that were without daughters asked them of God only with a view to consecrate them to him. In those days one would imagine that the young girls of every class in society considered virginity as their normal state, so common and, as it were, inborn among them, was the tendency to prefer virginity to marriage.‡

In conclusion, we may say, therefore, that parents do well in inclining their children at an early age to perfect chastity, and in employing for that purpose, not force, which would be very wrong, but Christian and gentle persuasion. St. Ambrose, in his "Exhortation to Virginity," bestows the highest praise on the widow Juliana, who, he relates, having lost her husband, overcame her grief, and gathering her children around her, said to them: "My dear children, you have lost your father. Faith alone is the inheritance of men, and the dowry of virgins. I advise you

---

* Amb., *De virginitate*, c. vii, nn. 35, 36. Ed. Migne.—Ventura, *Femme Catholique*, t. 2. p. 192.

† Darras, vol. 13. p. 452.   ‡ Ventura, ibid., p. 193.

to aim at what is loveliest on this earth: be angels among men. I have had experience of the troubles of a married life, and you see me deprived of the support of a husband and of the grace of virginity. My grief will be lighter, if I find in you what I have lost in myself; and if I am the mother of virgin children, I shall almost consider myself as having a claim to the same honor." * Her words were not in vain. Her son Lawrence entered the ranks of the clergy, and her daughters, three in number, embraced virginity, and observed it faithfully in their mother's home.†

They alone will not admire and envy the happiness of this holy widow, who do not understand the beauties of heroism. There are diseased eyes which the light fatigues: a feeble twilight is all that they can bear. So, alas! there are weak souls who cannot stand the broad effulgence of truth, nor the undimmed splendors of virtue.

---

* *Exhort. virg.*, c. iii, 4.
† *Admonitio in hunc librum.* Ed. Migne.

CHAPTER VII.

IS IT WRONG TO DISSUADE FROM PERFECT CHASTITY.

IF, in order to dissuade a person from celibacy, we were to say that marriage is something better than, or merely that it is as perfect as, celibacy, we would sin against faith. For, not only are we forbidden to give utterance to such statements, but we are, besides, not allowed to approve them, or give internal assent to them, short of a grievous sin and ceasing to belong to the Church. "Were it true that virginity or celibacy lies open to some reproaches, we ought, out of respect, abstain," says St. Chrysostom, "from making them known. He who vents contempt and outrage on the heroism that he cannot rival, justly incurs universal hatred, and passes in the eyes of the world for a senseless being and an enemy to virtue." "Woe to you," says the same doctor, in the words of Isaias,—" woe to you who call evil good, and good evil; who change darkness into light, and light into darkness, bitterness into sweetness, and sweetness into bitterness.

Now, what is there more lovely than virginity? What is better or more charming?"*

Afterward St. Chrysostom shows the sad consequences that may result from thoughtless and unscrupulous mockery of virginity or celibacy. Let us suppose, says he, that a man who has taken upon himself the severe sacrifices of virginity, should become with impunity the jest of great and small: whose courage, I ask, will not recoil from the prospect of taunts and ridicule? It is only a soul, superhumanly generous and noble, that could embrace a virtue so loaded with contempt. But allow others, less hardy and less skilled, to receive some mutual assistance from our encouragements.†

Still, as we have already noticed, while quoting a theologian whose authority is alleged by St. Liguori, parents may, for a good reason, such as the preservation of a family, invite their children to marry.‡ But if such action is permitted them for a serious reason, it would be sinful in these parents to have recourse to force, particularly when the children desire to follow a better career. Let us listen, in this matter, to the weighty authority of St. Thomas: "When a young man wishes to keep continence, his parents must not hinder him. It is written: 'Do not withhold him from doing good, who is able: if thou art

---

* *De virginitate*, capp. xx, xxi. † Ibid., c. xxii.
‡ St. Lig., *Theol. Mor.*, lib. 6, n. 850.

able, do good thyself also.' (Prov. iii, 27.) In cases of this nature we must fear to sadden or put out the Holy Ghost. It is a bad, not a good spirit, that guides him who resists the Holy Ghost. . . . When a soul, under the action of grace, has formed some salutary plan, it is a great cruelty to thwart its resolutions. It is malice like that of Herod, it is Babylonian barbarity, to slaughter newly-born infants; but greater still is the wickedness of men who crush in souls, even before birth, the holy desires which they have formed. Men of this kind seem to me worse than the infernal dragon standing up before the woman about to bring forth, and ready to devour her offspring as soon as it should come into the world."*

These words of St. Thomas ought to open the eyes of those who might be tempted to act inconsiderately, or through human respect, in the decisions they may be called on to give in reference to a state of life; but it is proper to enforce this doctrine by a striking example:—The youthful Demetrias was the daughter of the Consul Olibrius, surpassing in beauty, heiress to an immense fortune, and, as St. Jerome says, she occupied the first rank in the Roman world. The noblest alliances of the earth were open to her, but she would have no other spouse than the King of heaven. She ceased not to pray to God with many tears, begging of him so to dispose

---

* St. Th., opusc., *De eruditione principum*, lib. 5, c. xxx.

the hearts of her parents, that they would yield to her earnest desires. The time having come to disclose her magnanimous purpose, the young girl one day presented herself before Juliana, her mother, and her grandmother Proba; and, falling on her knees, besought both of them not to oppose her determination to belong entirely to the Lord. The only wish of Proba and Juliana was to see their dear child irrevocably consecrated to Jesus Christ. Full of the true spirit of the Gospel, these admirable women hastened to raise the young girl from her knees, trembling, as she was, with fear of offending them. They took her affectionately into their arms, covered her with kisses, and bedewed her with their tears. "God bless you, child," said they: "you will raise your family to still higher nobility, by conferring on it the glory of virginity." And that day was, for the house of Olibrius, the most delightful and the most joyous of feasts.*

The foregoing remarks will grow clearer by what we shall say later, when we shall treat of the religious state. We must now remove some prejudices against virginity that may take rise in Christian minds. Men indeed change, but the Spirit of lies always spreads the same errors among them. The objections, therefore, against virginity, of a Helvidius, of a Jovinian, and of the

---

* Ventura, *Femme Catholique;* St. Jerome, *Epist. ad Demetriad. de servanda virginitate.*

Protestants, though a hundred times overthrown by the doctors of the Church, are still upon the lips of some worldlings of our own day. It is important, then, to bring their nothingness fully into light, so as to rescue the faithful from their dangerous influence.

Were all to observe celibacy or virginity, the human race would become extinct! This objection has been urged by the impious Rousseau. St. Jerome refuted it long ago in his controversy with Jovinian: "Have no fear: society will not disappear through excessive zeal for chastity. That virtue is rare, because it is arduous. Many are called to it, but only a few are chosen."*

Alas! the Church by the voice of her ministers incessantly preaches the observance of God's commandments: will she ever persuade the greater number of men not to transgress them? Now, if many neglect to practise what is essential for salvation, is there any motive to fear that all will take to observing what is only a counsel? The ruin of society will come from another quarter. It will come from the vice that depopulates families. Multiply virgins, and marriages will be chaste and fruitful. The example of virgins will be an exhortation to the married. Besides, celibacy exacts no dowry: parents will consequently be less in dread of a numerous offspring, when they have the hope that some of their children,

---

* *Hieron. adv. Jovinian.*, lib. 1, c. i, n. 36.

by following a life of celibacy, will leave the paternal inheritance whole and entire to their brothers or sisters. In this we only express the thought of SS. Chrysostom and Ambrose. Who ever sought a wife and did not find her? said the latter to his slanderers. And we might add: If there are young women who have not found husbands, is the blame to be laid at the door of perfect chastity? But rather let us listen to the illustrious prelate of Milan: " Where there is greatest zeal for virginity, there also is the greatest number of men. Every year more virgins are consecrated to God in Africa, and in the churches of the East and of Alexandria, than there are men born in Italy."* A mother may say: I married, and my children must also marry. She is not wrong in speaking thus if her children, of their own free will, choose to embrace the marriage state; but if they desire to follow a higher call, why should obstacles be thrown in their way? St. Chrysostom cannot understand how parents, who have experience of the coldness and hollowness of earthly pleasures, can still make efforts to thrust their children into them.† St. Jerome asks the mother who insists on making her daughter marry because she herself married, why she is so envious of that child. She has, says he, been nourished at your breast,

---

* Chrysost., *De virginitate*, c. xviii; Amb., *De virginitate*, c. vii, n. 35. † *Adversus oppugnantes vitam monast.*, c. xv.

and you grow angry because she refuses the common soldier in order to be the bride of the King himself? Her resolution is an immense glory for you; through her you will be allied to Jesus Christ.*

But we wish to see our children's children! This is an objection which St. Chrysostom puts to himself, and here is his answer: "In the first place, it is not sure that marriage will result in children. Should it bestow any on you, so much the greater will be the annoyances of parents; for the joy which children bring cannot be compared with the anxiety and constant care which they require, and the fears which they excite."† When we give up the world, what gain is it that some one should bear our name after us? said a philosophic pagan mentioned by St. Jerome. What comfort will it be for us in our old age to be obliged to support some one that perhaps will die before us, or will be the torment of our days by his bad conduct; or, again, may, as he grows up, regret that our life does not come to an earlier end? Our best and our safest heirs are the friends and parents that we can choose according to our pleasure, and not those we have to bear, and who may turn to every bad use what we acquired by much toil and hardship.‡

---

* *Ad Eustoch.*, c. xx. † St. Chrysost., lib. 3, c. xvi.
‡ *Adv Jovinian.*, lib. 1, c. xlvii.

Were any to say that celibacy is barren and without honor, we would reply that the most faithful life is one spent in devotedness and works of self-sacrifice. That was not a barren life which Epaminondas led, who observed celibacy in order to serve his country better, and assured those who advised him to marry, "I leave as heir to my name the victory of Leuctra." It were easy to show, to any one that is willing to open his eyes, celibacy, in the course of Christian ages, sending apostles into the Old and the New World, evangelizing the poor, teaching children, building hospitals, taking care of the sick, and, as a ministering angel in families, ever ready with consolation where there is a tear to be dried, or any holy work to be done. Ever since Christ and his blessed Mother gave it a consecration, celibacy has been a source of confusion to those alone for whom, as Bernard says, confusion is glory.* How many lives would have passed away in obscurity, had not celibacy flung its splendors around them! How many humble maidens, who would have been only little known married women, became, through the self-sacrifice of celibacy, the love and admiration, not of one poor village or town, but of large cities and entire countries! Look at Joan of Arc who saved France, and is now one of its highest glories!

---

*S. Bern. *ad Sophiam Virg.*, epist. 113.

When the illustrious Demetrias, of whom we have already had occasion to speak, consecrated herself to God, the farthest bounds of the East, says St. Jerome, were astir at this prodigy, and the cities bordering on the Mediterranean took part in this triumph of Christian glory. Was there a mother, O Juliana! who did not proclaim thee blest? Unbelievers look upon future goods as uncertain; but in fixing thy hopes upon them, thou, O virgin! hast received more than thou hast given away. As the wife of a man, thou wouldst have been known by one province; but all the earth has resounded with the fame of the virgin of Christ.*

We are well aware that there may be men who are the disgrace of the celibacy which they profess; but, were we to judge of a state of life by the conduct of those who dishonor it, what condition could we esteem, what state could we embrace? Besides, the shortcomings of those living in Christian celibacy might often pass for virtues, if placed alongside the sins of the worldling. Poor slaves of the world! the Christian maiden whom you laugh at has no contempt for you; she sacrifices herself, she weeps and prays earnestly for you. If, at any future day, the pure light of truth should break in upon you, it is to her that you will owe it.

---

* Hieron., *Epist. ad Demetriad. de virginitate servanda*, 6.

Paragraph 2.—*Virginity.*

All that has been said on the possibility, the advantages, and the excellence of celibacy, is applicable to the state of virginity. We shall not here go over that ground again. However, we shall speak a little of virginity, so as not to appear to mention, only in a passing way, what is, according to St. Ambrose, a leading virtue.*

---
* St. Thom., 2, 2, q. 152, a. 3; Ambr., *De virginitate*, lib. 1, c. i.

CHAPTER I.

THE VIRTUE OF VIRGINITY.

VIRGINITY, says the Angelical, is a special virtue whereby we keep, and determine always to keep, ourselves free from every sinful pleasure. The fixed renunciation of all that is contrary to virginity deserves praise on account of its end, which ought to be a readier devotion of one's self to the things of God. Virginity, materially considered, consists in an integrity of body unsullied by any wilful stain. When viewed as a virtue, it implies a vow always to maintain that integrity. Children at their birth possess the material part of this virtue; but they have not the resolution to forever keep this integrity for God's sake, which resolution properly constitutes the virtue of virginity.* Those who have never done anything that could make them forfeit virginity, but have not resolved to retain it forever, are virgins in body; but they have not the virtue of virginity, which has its seat in the soul.

The virtue of virginity is lost even by the desire to do anything that would offend against bodily integrity.† "Of what use is it for the body to keep pure," says St. Chrysostom, "if the nobler

---

* St. Thom., 2, 2, q. 152, a. 3; Ambr., *De virginitate*, lib. I, c. i.
† Hieron. *ad Eustoch.: Perit et mente virginitas*, epist. 22, n. 5.

nature of the virgin, namely, her soul, has lost the splendor of virginity? If the temple is in ruins, to what purpose do the barriers that surround it remain standing? When the throne is stained, what is the good of keeping clean the place where it rests? It is not by his hair, his staff, or his cloak, we recognize a philosopher, but by his actions and his thoughts. It is not arms and a belt that make a soldier, but strength and courage. Would it not, therefore, be ludicrous to make the virgin's virtue consist in simplicity of dress or modesty of countenance, without looking into the depths of her soul and penetrating into her most secret thoughts?"*

The formal part of virginity, or the virtue that resides in the soul, may, when lost, be recovered by repentance, according to the teaching of St. Thomas.† That is to say, when virginity of body has not been forfeited, guilty desires can be expiated by penance, and we may still practise the virtue of virginity. A man who intended to spend his fortune foolishly, but who has it still, may recall his silly intentions, and employ his wealth in abundant alms or in practising the virtue of munificence. But if he has squandered all that he owned, he may repent to no end: his sorrow will not restore him his lost goods, and he will remain incapable of generosity to the poor.

---

* Chrysost., *De virginitate*, c. vi, 7.
† St. Th., 2, 2, q. 152, a. 3, ad 3.

In like manner, observes St. Thomas, he, who through sin has lost virginity of body, can no longer, even by repentance, recover the matter of virginity: all he can get back is the resolution or determination to be a virgin.* "God, who can do all things," wrote St. Jerome to Eustochium, " cannot restore a virgin that has fallen; he can deliver her from the chastisement which she deserves, but he will not crown her who has profaned her body by sin."†

If you lose the treasure of entire chastity, wrote the eloquent author of the work on " True Virginity," whatever you may do afterward, even though you should run over land and sea, go down into the abysses or rise into the immensity of the heavens, you will never be able to retrieve your loss. Indeed, how can that which has once been foul, become like what has always been without spot? Sin will undoubtedly be remitted through repentance; but the soul sullied by sin, unable to become as one that never was tarnished, will have to lament her misfortune as long as she dwells in this life.‡ Tears of repentance, however, must be attended with trust in the mercy of God. For those who cannot practise virginity, there yet remains celibacy, or continence, whose value and excellence we have previously mentioned.

---

* St. Th., 2, 2, q. 152, a. 3, ad 3.   † Epist. 22.
‡ *De vera virginitate, inter opera S. Basilii,* tom. 2, n. 59.

CHAPTER II.

GLORY OF VIRGINITY.

THE learned Cornelius à Lapide enumerates the prerogatives of virginity. The first is, that virgins compose the angelic family which Christ came to set upon earth. He who was adored by angels in heaven, says St. Jerome, wished to have angels in this world also.* "Men and women who keep virginity are angels, and not of a common kind, but of a very high and noble class. Free from the bonds of the flesh, the heavenly spirits observe virginity in the kingdom of God. Standing near the throne of the Lord of the universe, they are in a place and of a nature that save them from the slightest stain. But the virgins of earth are still more astonishing in their virtue and angelic purity; for they practise them against the assaults of Satan and the evil tendencies of our fallen nature."† St. John Chrysostom uses similar language.‡

But there is still another glory of virginity. In the words of St. Ambrose, it sought in heaven

---

* Corn. in 1 Cor. vii, 34. Hieron. *ad Eustoch.*, epist. 22.
† *De vera virginitate, inter opera S. Basilii*, tom. 2, n. 51.
‡ *Homil. fest. S. Aloys. Gonz.* (Brev. Rom.)

for what it was to copy on earth. It rose above the skies, the heavens, the stars, and the angels, to reach the Word of God in the bosom of his Father.*

A third glory of virginity is that, according to St. Jerome, it is a wholeburnt offering. And, indeed, it gives up and consecrates the soul and the body of man to God and to heavenly things.†

In the fourth place, the virgin is the spouse of Jesus Christ. "The virgin is wedded to the Lord," exclaims the most eloquent doctor of the Greek Church. "When that is said, all that remains for us is silence, for nothing can surpass that dignity. She who marries a king looks upon herself as the happiest of women: but should you not, virgins, make every sacrifice, even that of life itself, were it necessary, to please Him whom you have chosen? He is no man of earth, he is no slave: he is the God who reigns in the heavens. He is above every principality and power; above every virtue and name that can be spoken. He spreads out the heavens, he shakes the earth, the cherubim fall down before him, he is inaccessible to the seraphim, but for you he is a spouse, and even more than a spouse."‡ Nor is this blessed union barren, it is rich in fruit; but its fruits are spiritual, not corporal. Its fruits are virtues: alms and other works of charity,—holy

---

* Corn., 1 Cor. vii, 34; Ambr., *De virginitate*, lib. I, c. iii.
† Corn., ibid., et Hieron., Brev. in Ps. 95.
‡ *De cohabit. illicit.*

examples by which virgins bring and beget other souls to Jesus Christ.*

Fifthly, Jesus Christ loves virgins, first, as his spouses. If the virgin is careful to please our Lord, she must know how eager he is to please his spouse. The woman, who has chosen a mortal man as the guide and guardian of her life, receives, in return for her care and submission, the advice and continual assistance of her husband. Far more so the virgin, as a reward for her zeal to please God, can always rely on the paternal watchfulness of Providence, to whose hands she has confided, with fullest trust, the entire care of her life."† History, in relating to us all the torments of virgins in the first persecutions of the Church, also informs us that none of these glorious martyrs was ever dishonored. Lions fell prostrate before Thecla when she was abandoned to their fury; and more than once angels descended from heaven to shield the virtue of the spouses of Christ.‡ Again, Jesus Christ loves virgins as his choicest soldiers.§ "In a battle," says St. Chrysostom, "every one does not occupy indifferently any place whatever. Some are stationed in the wings, some in the centre of the army. Others are the special body-guard of the king, and go wherever he goes. It is the same with the body of virgins. A band of men,

---

* Corn. in 1 Cor. vii, 34.
† Ibid., *Basil. de vera virginitate*, n. 24. ‡ Ibid. in 1 Cor. vii, 35.
§ Corn., ibid.; Ambr., *De virginibus*, lib. I, c. iii.

brilliant with gold and decorations, do not point more surely to the presence of the monarch than virgins tell of the presence of Christ. The former encircle the royal carriage; but virgins, like the cherubim of heaven, are the royal carriage, and, as the seraphim, they form, at the same time, its beautiful escort."*

Sixthly, virgins are the glory of Christianity, the most distinguished portion of the flock of Christ, the richest jewels and ornaments of the Church. For this reason, St. Ambrose teaches that virginity is a mark, a characteristic, of the true religion.† Unbelievers may admire virginity, but only the Church of God, says St. Chrysostom, has put it in practice.‡

Furthermore, in heaven virgins shall enjoy a special reward, and wear a remarkable crown.§ The virgin is a queen in heaven, though perhaps on earth she was a slave, despised, ignorant, poor, and an outcast. Jesus Christ gives her not only a glorious immortality, but he clothes her as his spouse in a robe of surpassing splendor.‖

"O virgins!" exclaims St. Augustine, "you will appear at the nuptials of the Lamb, singing a new canticle, and playing on your harps. That canticle is not the one which the rest of men sing. You alone know its strains. In heaven virgins follow the Lamb whithersoever he goes.

---

* Chrysost., *De cohabit. illicit.*, lib. 2, 6.
† Corn. in 1 Cor. vii, 35, ibid.   ‡ *De virginitate*, c. i.
§ Cornel., ibid.   ‖ *De vera virginitate, inter op. S. Basil.*, n. 26.

And where does the Lamb go? What is that place into which none but you even dare to follow him? What are those bowers, those lovely fields? Indeed, joy is the vesture of that home of delights; not the vain, silly, and treacherous joy of this present life, nor even the joy experienced in heaven by those who have practised virginity. Your joys are different from all others. Wheresoever the Lamb goes, you shall follow him on account of your virginity of body and of soul. And, in truth, to follow is to imitate. Others may imitate his poverty or his humility, you alone can imitate his virginity. Behold that Lamb! he has run a virginal career. How can they follow him who have lost what can never be recovered? Follow him, guarding perseveringly what you have vowed to him with so much generosity. Unable to follow him, the multitude of the faithful will see you forming his escort. They will see you, but without envy; they will rejoice to behold in you what they themselves do not possess."*

Having explained the glories of virginity, Cornelius à Lapide ends with these words, which it is important to note: " All these prerogatives," says he, " belong as well to virgins living in their families as to those who dwell in a convent. There were no convents in the days of St. Paul or of St. Ignatius the Martyr. Hence, when they praised

---
* *De sancta virgin.*, c. xxvii.

virginity, their eulogies were given to virgins that lived in the houses of their parents." We may also remark with St. Clement that the nobler name and the higher place in heaven are promised to virgins of either sex, namely: to men as well women.* We shall close the subject of virginity with the words of St. Chrysostom: "I have shown you all the excellence of virginity; I have explained to you all its advantages; you are now free to make choice of it. I do not attempt to force you against your will to the practice of virtue."†

Paragraph 3.—Widowhood.

Virginity, says Bossuet, is an angelic state; widowhood follows close upon it.‡ Let us say a few words on this condition of life.

It is certain that persons in widowhood are allowed to marry again. To condemn second marriages would be to lapse into the errors of the Montanists. Listen to the teaching of the Apostle of the Gentiles: "But I say to the unmarried and to the widows, it is good for them if they so continue, even as I. But if they do not contain themselves, let them marry. For it is better to marry than to be burnt" (by the fire of temptation). "A woman, if her husband die, is

---

* *Epist. ad virgines*, c. iv.
† *De virginitate*, c. lxxvi.   See also *La virginité*, by the Abbé Coulin.   ‡ Bossuet, Lettre 83. Ed. Martin Beaupré.

at liberty: let her marry to whom she will; only in the Lord "—that is, according to the law and fear of God, as à Lapide explains these words. " But more blessed shall she be if she so remain," either in this world in which her life will be more quiet and holy, or in heaven, says the same commentator, where her happiness and glory will be greater.* From these words of the apostle, which are in themselves so clear, we must infer that second marriages would be obligatory on persons living a sinful life in widowhood, and unwilling to employ any other means of amendment or preservation. Outside, however, of this case, and of a few others that are very rare, second, third, and even eighth marriages, as St. Jerome has it, are neither commanded nor forbidden. Strictly speaking, they are not even matter of counsel: they are merely allowable. Widowhood is a state happier and better than marriage; it falls, therefore, under the counsels. Such is the teaching of St. Paul: it is also that of the fathers, from whom we shall adduce some passages:—

"We do not prohibit second marriages," says St. Ambrose, " but, on the other hand, we do not advise them; for not all that is allowed is profitable. The widow has no command to remain a widow, but she is counselled to do so; and the counsel has not only been once given, but has been often repeated. Do not say: 'I am without

---

* St. Paul, 1 Cor. vii, et Corn., ibid.

assistance.' This is the customary excuse of her who wishes to re-marry. Neither should you say: 'I am all alone.' Loneliness is favorable to purity; the modest woman loves retirement; she who is not so, is anxious to go out and parade herself. You have, you say, business to transact? And are there no lawyers in the world? But you are in dread of enemies? Well, then, our Lord himself pleads your case before the judges, and says to them: 'Deal justly with the widow.' You are anxious to save your property? Chastity is also a property of the very highest value, and the widow keeps it far better than the married woman. But still you wish to get married? You are allowed to do so. I make no inquiries with regard to your motives: why do you dissemble when giving them? If your reasons are virtuous, state them; if otherwise, be silent about them. Accuse neither your relatives, nor God, when you complain of want of support; do not say you marry for the sake of your children, while depriving them of a mother.

"There are things, allowable in themselves, which age sanctions no longer. Why prepare for the wedding of the mother during or after the wedding of the daughter? What is that woman lately married who yet has sons-in-law, and who, by a second husband, will have children younger than her nephews?"* Again the widow says,

---

* St. Amb., *De viduis*, c. xi.

Who will bring up my children? "Alas!" answers St. Jerome, "they allege, as reason for their marriage, the very thing that ought to prevent them from doing so; for, by her second marriage, the widow places over her children, not a father who will provide for them, but an enemy. If you have children, why marry again? And if you have none, does not experience teach you to fear a like barrenness in the future?"*

The world itself understands these ideas, and St. Jerome gives numerous examples of noble pagan ladies, who, having lost their husbands, preferred death to the bonds of a second marriage.†

St. Ambrose spoke to middle-aged persons: St. Chrsyostom wrote chiefly for young widows. He says: "I consider it useless to speak to women advanced in years, and who, nevertheless, are thinking of a second marriage. Could any words of mine convince them, when neither years, nor age, nor experience has been able to make them forego their purpose? Hence, I speak to young widows. We go on cheerfully with an enterprise whose beginnings have been favorable; but if we fail at the outset, we give up everything. Therefore, a young widow, it seems to me, ought to be all the further from a second marriage, because she has known sorrow and widowhood so early in life. In remaining a widow, she is sure of her future, and protects herself against

---

* St. Hieron., Epist. 51, n. 15.   † *Adv. Jovinian.*, lib. I, c. xliii.

similar misfortunes. Though the state of widowhood is the same for all widows, the rewards differ widely, and are more brilliant for some than for others. The widow who, while yet young, undergoes the yoke of continence, deserves more honor and glory than another who takes up the practice only in her old age." *

The heavenly rewards promised to widowhood, and of which St. Chrysostom speaks, have at all times made some noble souls, whom the world sought to wrest from God, persevere faithfully in that holy state of life. A high-born Roman lady, named Marcella, lost her husband, seven months after her marriage. The high rank of her family, her youth, her personal beauty, and her many virtues, induced a Roman consul called Cerialis, already advanced in years, to seek her hand, with a promise to leave her all his property. Albina, Marcella's mother, urged her daughter to accept the brilliant offer. "If I wanted to marry," replied Marcella, "instead of devoting the remainder of my life to perpetual chastity, I would look for a husband, and not for a fortune." Cerialis told her that sometimes men of a certain age live a long time, whereas young men die very soon. "It is true," said Marcella, "that young men *may* not live long, but it is sure that old men *can* not live long." And she continued

---

* St. Chrysost., "Second Treatise against Second Marriages." Migne vol. 1, coll. 618, 619.

to live on, in her widowhood, amid the practices of piety.*

St. Gregory relates that, in the time of Theodoric, King of the Goths, the noble and youthful Galla, daughter of the consul and patrician Symmachus, was married, in the flower of her years, to a husband every way worthy of her. Within a year she had the misfortune to lose him. Her worldly rank, wealth, and beauty seemed to call her to a second marriage; nor were there wanting busy people to urge upon her such a step. Even physicians plied her with reasons of their own; but nothing could shake the resolution of Galla. The second marriage to which she looked forward was that which is contracted with God. It begins in sorrow, but it ends in everlasting joy; while the unions of the world take place in the midst of noisy rejoicings, and close in tears.

All Rome was a witness of the struggle between God and the world in the soul of the illustrious widow. "Galla," says St. Gregory, "laid aside her splendid attire and the ornaments of the world, to give herself up to God in a monastery near the basilica of the blessed apostle, St. Peter. There she lived for many years in great simplicity of heart, engaged in constant prayer and the practice of exhaustless charity."† There, too, she closed her earthly career by a holy death.

---

* Corn. à Lapide in 1 Tim. v, 5.
† St. Greg., Magn. Dial., lib. 4, c. xiii, ed. Migne, col. 340.

SECT. II.—THE STATE OF PERFECTION.

INTRODUCTORY REMARKS.

What is Perfection, and what is the State of Perfection.

We have run through the several conditions of the common Christian life, and now we have reached the state of perfection. Henceforth our task will be an easy one. We have only to draw from the abundant materials which St. Thomas, St. Liguori, and Suarez have accumulated for us. We shall begin by stating what perfection is, and making a clear distinction between it and the state of perfection. Following in the footsteps of St. Thomas, Suarez, says: " Theologians place the perfection of Christian life in the perfection of charity. This is also the theory of the holy fathers. The reason of it is this: what constitutes the perfection of a thing is its union with its last end. Now, our last end is God known by faith; our perfection, therefore, consists in union with God. But it is charity that unites us to him. Through it we bind ourselves closely to God, and become one spirit with him, as St. Paul expresses it, and as St. John points out in these words: " He that abideth in charity, abideth in God, and God in him." (1 John iv, 16.) St. Prosper says that charity is the strongest of all affections. Hence it unites us to God more forcibly than any other; and in this life we cannot be more bound to him by anything than by love, because charity tends to God considered in himself, it subjects man to him in a wonderful manner, and makes him conformable to his ever-adorable will. Wherefore the entire perfection of the Christian life is in charity.* Still, charity is not so all-sufficing for perfection, as to include everything else. Other virtues must accompany it and rest upon it.†

In this life perfect charity can exist in two ways. First, in so far as it banishes from the heart of man all that is opposed to charity, as, for instance, mortal sin. Without this perfection, charity is out of the question, and therefore it is required for salvation. Secondly, perfect charity may exist in this life, in the sense that it excludes from the soul of man, not simply what is opposed to charity, but whatever also hinders the soul from going fully to God.‡

Viewed in the first light, this perfection of charity is said to be essential;§ it supposes that we love nothing above, against, or more than God.‖ It requires in the soul a disposition to keep all the commandments.¶ Jesus Christ speaks of this perfection where he says to all men: "Be ye perfect as your heavenly Father is perfect."** This essential perfection concerns the common

---

* Suarez, *De statu perfectionis*, lib. 1, c. iii, nn. 4, 5. † Ibid
‡ St. Th., 2, 2, q. 184, a. 2.   § Suar., lib. 1, c. x, n. 1.
‖ St. Th., 2, 2, q. 184, a. 3 ad 2.   ¶ Suar., ibid., c. iv, n. 17.
** Ibid. c. x, n. 1; et Matt. v, 48.

Christian life, of which we have hitherto spoken, For, though all who are in that state have not attained this degree of perfection, since many do not comply with the duties of Christianity, and consequently are void of spiritual life, nevertheless all are in a state where they are bound to aim at and acquire this perfection, and they are supplied with ample means to reach it.*

The perfection of charity taken from the second point of view, that is, in so far as excluding, not only mortal sin, but all that prevents the soul from belonging entirely to God, may be called accidental. It is a better and more profitable degree, and it is of it that our Lord speaks when saying, "If thou wilt be perfect, go sell all thou hast."† It is this loftier degree of holiness that is commonly called perfection.

Now, this perfection of the Christian life cannot be acquired unless a man practises, first, the commandments, and, in the next place, some of the counsels. This proposition is certain, and is generally taught by theologians. However, such as are not in the state of perfection may perform some works of counsel, and thus spontaneously come to perfection, without being held to it by their condition of life.‡ Still, strictly speaking, a person is not in a state of perfection by the mere fact of being in perfect charity; he reaches

---

* Suar., c. x, n. 2.
† Ibid., n. 1 ; et c. iv, n. 14, et Matt. xix, 21
‡ Suar., c. v, n. 2, et c. x, n. 4.

perfection only by binding himself in a special manner, and with a certain solemnity, to it, and to what pertains to perfection.*

We may, then, be perfect and not be in a state of perfection, and be in a perfect state without being perfect. Hence, the state of perfection is not to be confounded with perfection itself. With regard to perfection, the state of perfection is as a means with respect to an end. It may be defined: A fixed and permanent mode of life, established to acquire or practise the perfection of Christian life. This mode must be visible; for the state of perfection is not for angels, but for human beings. It must, then, consist in acts that can be known by men and by the visible Church of Christ; so that, even though one were to bind himself by secret vow to serve God in a perfect way, that would not be enough to place him in a state of perfection properly so called.†

Christian perfection calls far more for the observance of the commandments than of the counsels. The state of perfection tends to the full practice of both, though it has especially in view the commandments, as being more essential to salvation.‡ Nevertheless, that state is constituted by the counsels. For, to keep, and resolve always to keep, the commandments, would not put one in a state of perfection: the state must

---

* St. Th., 2, 2, q. 181, a. 4. † Suar., lib. I, c. v.
‡ Ibid., c. v; et c. x, n. 6.

be constituted by an act superadded to what is of precept, and consequently by an act belonging to the counsels.*

Having now given as clear an idea as we could of the nature and state of perfection, we say, with Suarez, that it divides itself into a state of perfection to be acquired, and a state of perfection to be practised; or, in other equivalent terms, in perfection there is the state of those who are tending to it, and the state of those who are already perfect. The characteristic of the state of aspiration or tendency is to effect the salvation of those who embrace it; and the characteristic of the state of those who exercise perfection is zeal for the salvation of their neighbor.†

We shall treat in turn of the one and of the other.

ARTICLE I.

The State of Tendency to Perfection, or the Religious State.

"The religious state," says Suarez, "is nothing but a tendency to perfection."‡ According to the common usage of the Church, the name, religious state, taken in an exact meaning, indicates the perfect state of regulars, who consecrate and give themselves entirely to God by taking

---

* Suar., lib. 1, c. xi, n. 12. † Ibid., c. xiv, n. 3.
‡ Ibid., lib. 2, Prolog.

the three vows of the three chief counsels, that is, of obedience, poverty and chastity, in an approved religious society. When taken in a broader sense, the religious state comprises other modes of life that men adopt by voluntarily devoting themselves to the worship and service of God, and binding themselves to keep certain counsels.* What we are about to say will have special reference to the religious state strictly and properly so called. Having briefly spoken of its origin, its excellence, and its advantages, we shall inquire whether it is of precept or of counsel, and whether a person may vow to embrace it. After that we shall see whether it is allowable to exhort persons to enter religion, and whether it is forbidden to dissuade them from doing so. Lastly, we shall treat of the chief impediments to entrance into religion, and answer certain questions connected with them. On all these points we shall advance nothing that is not supported by the authority of the most celebrated doctors and theologians of the Church.

---

* Suar., lib. 2, c. i, n. 1.

CHAPTER I.

ORIGIN OF THE RELIGIOUS STATE.

"Although," says Suarez, "we find in the Old Law a shadow and, as it were, a rough sketch of the religious state, however, its perfection and complete formation are the work of the law of grace. It was fitting that Jesus Christ, when coming from heaven to earth in order to bring mankind a new law and more copious graces, should teach and set up in his Church a new mode of life calculated to lead men more efficaciously to perfection. And this is what he has done. The religious state, in its essential elements, was given to men and instituted directly by Christ himself; so that it is of divine right, not in the sense that God makes it imperative, but that he gives it as a counsel. This is the view of all Catholics whose views are correct and sound.*

This truth is supported by the fathers. Their common teaching is that Jesus Christ has divided the lives of Christians into two classes. In the one, are those who follow the common road of

---

* Suar., lib. 3, c. i, nn. 5, 6 ; et c. ii, nn. 3, 4.

the commandments; and in the other, those who profess a higher and an almost angelic life, that is, the religious state. For instance, St. Basil says that, by the words, " Come to me all ye that labor," Christ calls us to the religious life.* But the chief basis of the doctrine is the Gospel. In it Christ, indeed, exhorts men to practise the three evangelical counsels, and to take and keep perpetual vows. And as these three vows constitute the substance of the religious life, this manner of living has therefore been established by Christ himself.†

To bring the point into fuller light, let us, following St. Thomas and Suarez, speak of the evangelical counsels, which, considered in their object, are three in number: that is, the counsels of chastity, poverty, and obedience.‡ They are called evangelical counsels, because Jesus Christ was the first to give them. They are also called counsels of perfection, or simply counsels. They are proper to the religious state.§

It is true, as Suarez teaches, that they may be practised and vowed outside of convents; still they form, as we shall soon see, the essence of the religious life properly so called.

---

* Suar., lib. 3, c. ii, n. 4. † Ibid., n. 5. ‡ Ibid., lib. 1, c. viii.
§ Ibid., nn. 3, 6.

CHAPTER II.

EVANGELICAL COUNSELS.

These counsels are obligatory upon no one, as we shall explain later; yet we may ask whether they are addressed to every one. We have heard Cornelius à Lapide and the catechism of the Council of Trent teaching that perfect chastity is counselled to all men.* Does the same hold for the counsels of poverty and obedience?

Our blessed Lord said to a young man: "If thou wilt be perfect, go sell all thou hast." To elude these words, the heretic Osiander used to say that Jesus Christ had, indeed, counselled poverty to that young man, but had not done so to all men. "But," replies Suarez, "this assertion is gratuitous, and owes its origin solely to the obstinacy of him who makes it. For, why is such a counsel salutary for that young man, unless its object is in itself better and more profitable? Moreover, Jesus Christ said, besides, to the young man at the same time: 'If thou wilt enter into life, keep the commandments;' and these other words: 'If thou wilt be perfect, go sell all thou

---

* Sect. I, art. 2, c. i. Also Bellarm., *De membris ecclesiæ*, lib. 2, c. ix.

hast.' Now, the first portion was spoken, not for the young man alone, but for all men; therefore so was the second." And the learned theologian concludes thus: "It is for all rich people an excellent counsel to love poverty, so as to shun the dangers attendant on riches."*

Having shown that the counsel of obedience is contained in the words, "Follow me," addressed by our Lord to the young man, Suarez remarks that many of our Lord's words apply to all, and should not be restricted to the few who were present when he spoke, but are extended to whoever wishes to follow the evangelical counsels; and since the object of the counsel of obedience is of importance for all the faithful, the words of our Lord which convey this counsel are addressed to every one.†

St. Thomas is still more explicit than Suarez. "We ought," says he, "to receive the words of our Lord handed down to us in Scripture, as if we heard them spoken by our Lord himself. Has he not said to his apostles, 'And what I say to you, I say to all: Watch'? (Mark xiii, 37.) And St. Paul tells us: 'What things soever were written, were written for our learning.' (Rom. xv, 4.)" Hereupon St. John Chrysostom comments as follows: "Had Jesus Christ spoken only for those who listened to him, his words would

---

* Suar., lib. 8, c. ii, n. 4; et Matt. xix, 17, 21.
† Suar., lib. 10, c. i, n. 18.

not have been written. They were spoken for the first disciples, but they were written for us. It is clear, then, that the words of Holy Scripture are addressed, not to those only who stood by when these words were delivered, but to all the faithful who are to live in the long course of ages."

But let us examine in particular whether the counsel of our Lord, "Go sell all thou hast" (Matt. xix, 21), was not given only to the young man to whom Jesus Christ addressed the words, or whether it was delivered for all men. Let us reflect on what follows. In the same chapter St. Peter says: "Behold, we have left all things and have followed thee" (v. 27); then our Lord promises a general reward: "And every one that hath left house, or brethren, or sisters, or father, or mother, or wife, or children, or lands for my name's sake, shall receive an hundredfold, and shall possess life everlasting" (v. 29). Every one, therefore, can follow this counsel just as if he heard our Saviour address it to him in person. Although he spoke to that particular young man, he gave the same counsel in a general way when he said: "If any man will come after me, let him deny himself, and take up his cross, and follow me." (Matt. xvi, 24.) Hereupon St. John Chrysostom says that our Lord spoke these words for all the world: If any one, that is, any man, or woman, if a king, if a freeman, if a slave, wishes! According to St. Basil, this complete denial of self is a forgetfulness of the past, and a giving-up of one's own will; and in this self-denial is included the renunciation of earthly goods. We must therefore accept the counsel given by our Lord to the young man as if our Lord himself addressed it to every one in particular.* This remarkable passage is wholly taken from St. Thomas.

But are the evangelical counsels possible? In treating of them, Suarez says that it is praiseworthy to vow any one of them and to keep it. Evidently, then, they are possible; for, according to all theologians, a vow with regard to an impossible thing is null, and has no binding force. "The gratitude we owe to God," adds the same Suarez, "does not lay on us a rigorous obligation to virginity, nor to the practice of poverty, nor to any other good works which are not commanded; although, if we wish to do anything of the kind out of gratitude to God, we are free to do it."† And here returns the reasoning of the learned commentator whom we take a delight in quoting: "Nothing is counselled save what is in the power and subject to the free will of man under God's grace,—a grace that God holds in readiness for, and bestows on, any one that asks for it."‡

---

* St. Th., opusc. 17, c. x.   † Suar., lib. I, c. ix, n. 21.
‡ Corn., Comment. in c. xix Matt.

To those who might fear that this beautiful and expansive doctrine of great theologians, while throwing open the path of perfection to generous souls, would depopulate the world, it were sufficient to recall what we have already said, and about which no one can entertain a doubt, namely: there is no hope that all the children of the Church will faithfully keep all the commandments. What apprehension, therefore, can there be that they will all turn to the practice of the evangelical counsels? The three counsels of poverty, chastity, and obedience, are indispensable and essential to the religious state, properly speaking: this is the teaching of St. Thomas, and all the theologians hold it with him.* The obligation always to practise these three counsels likewise belongs to the essence of the religious state; and this obligation is contracted by the vow which a person makes to God to keep them.†

Having settled this point, we now return to our subject, and repeat the reasoning of Suarez: "In the Gospel, Jesus Christ exhorts us to put in practice the three counsels of poverty, chastity, and obedience, and to take a perpetual vow to keep them. Now, the essence of the religious state consists in these three vows. Therefore, the religious state was established by Jesus Christ himself. If every one in particular of these counsels has been praised and commended

---

‡ Suar., lib. 2, c. ii, n. 3. § Ibid., c. iii.

by Jesus Christ, still more so has he exhorted us to keep them all; for the observance of one of them helps rather than hinders the observance of the others. Our blessed Lord intimated as much to us in the words, 'Go sell all thou hast, and come follow me.' For, by these words, he commands at once poverty and obedience, and necessarily supposes chastity: for, how could one freely follow Christ, if tied by the bonds of wedlock? Nor is it easy to combine poverty with the cares of a family."

Having quoted a number of passages from the Gospels in support of his thesis, Suarez concludes: "Jesus Christ has, then, clearly enough invited us to a state which fixes us permanently in the practice of the complete abnegation which he advises us to adopt. Our Lord has, therefore, instituted all that belongs to the substance of the religious state, even though he has not appointed or framed any particular rule. It was in the same way that he instituted the sacraments. He told us of their essentials, but he left to his Church the care of regulating everything accidental that pertains to them. I say, moreover," continues the same author, "that Christ established one religious institute in particular, by assembling a certain number of men, and laying down for them a peculiar mode of life. And, indeed, he called his apostles to a truly and properly called religious state. They really took the three vows of poverty, chastity and obedience; and they took these vows with a view to the state of perfection. Jesus Christ called them to a mixed form of life; that is, to a life both contemplative and active, and appointed as their special end the preaching of the Gospel. From the apostolic age down to our own day, the religious state has always been kept up in the Church. This is the common view of the fathers, and it is borne out by the history of the Church."*

---

* Suar., lib. 3, capp. ii et iii.

CHAPTER III.

EXCELLENCE OF THE RELIGIOUS STATE.

The religious state, so deserving of respect for its antiquity and divine origin, does not deserve less on account of its end, and the means it affords for the attainment of that end. To understand this matter, we must go back to principles that we have already mentioned.

"Every art," says Suarez, "has an object at which it aims. The state of perfection has its end, too, in view of which it bears with all its trials. This end is nothing more than the perfection of the Christian life."* " We have said, before, that the perfection of the Christian life is nothing more than the perfection of charity. However, the state of perfection has not solely in view the perfection of essential charity, which is common to all conditions of life, and which all Christians must possess who live up to their faith. The religious state has in view a perfect charity still greater and of higher excellence."†

" The perfection essential to all states requires in man a disposition to fulfil all the commandments of God, and it consists in the life of grace."‡

---

* Suar., lib. I, c. iii.   † Ibid., c. iv, n. 1   ‡ Ibid., n. 4.

"The profession of Christianity is ordained to enable man to reach, at least, that amount of perfection, and it supplies the means necessary and sufficient for that object. It is true that those who are in the common state, that is, in the world, have it in their power to perform works of supererogation, and, with God's grace, to grow as much as they choose in Christian perfection; but their condition of life does not bind them to do so; nor does it furnish them any special means therefor." *

"The state of perfection, and the religious state in particular, has also chiefly in view the fulfilment of the commandments. Next to the full remission of sin, the most important requisite for salvation is the preservation of grace and the avoidance of mortal sin. And because this twofold work is very hard for fallen nature, a state has been opened in which the occasions of sin are fewer, and the danger of losing grace less formidable: and this is one of the purposes of the state of perfection." †

"Add to what has already been said, that the state of perfection, and consequently the religious state, has for end, not only the keeping of the commandments,—that is to say, the avoidance of mortal sin, which is absolutely indispensable for salvation,—but it aims, besides, at the complete observance of precepts which shut out as far

---

‡ Suar., lib. I, c. ii, n. 9.   § Ibid., c. i, n. 9.

as possible even venial sins, because that degree of perfection is more necessary and peremptory than the keeping of the counsels."*

Finally, the perfection aimed at by the religious state consists in a desire to do the will of God, not only as manifested in the commandments, but also as pointed out to us by the counsels.†

What a sublime purpose! The religious state has for its aim to beget in men, even in this life, a disposition similar to that of the blessed in heaven. It seeks to establish the reign of God in its fulness here on earth, and to have the adorable will of the Lord done in this world as it is done in heaven itself.

But, in every wisely planned state, the means appointed for the attainment of its end must be in keeping with the end itself. Now, the state of perfection, or the religious state, has in view a degree of virtue higher than the charity which is imperative on all, and which consists in the fulfilment of the commandments. The religious state, therefore, must supply the soul with helps for perfection of a far nobler nature than are to be found in the common state of the commandments. For this very reason, too, it must, besides the keeping of the commandments, insist on and require the practice of the counsels. ‡ And so it does. We have seen that every one of the counsels promised to God by vow pertains to

---

* Suar., lib. I, c. i, n. 11. † Ibid., c. iv, n. 16. ‡ Ibid., c. x, n. 5

the substance of the perfect religious life. And these three counsels, according to St. Thomas, remove everything that could hinder man from tending fully to God. For they do away with, in the first place, the desire of worldly possessions, by the vow of poverty; secondly, sensual enjoyments, by the vow of chastity; and, lastly, the disorders of self-will, which are repressed by the vow of obedience. Moreover, the cares of the world, which choke desire for perfection, arise, first, from the management of earthly goods: but this source of anxiety is put an end to by poverty; in the next place, from the responsibilities of a family: and this the religious is freed from by his vow of chastity; thirdly, from the direction of one's own actions: and obedience rids us of all anxiety on this head.

What we say here is scarcely anything more than a translation of the words of St. Thomas in his "Sum of Theology."* The treasures that we find in it make us admire the perfection of the means which the religious state possesses for the attainment of its end; and they display the wisdom of God who has established that state for the perfection of the children of his holy Church. But there is something besides this. St. Thomas adds that the three vows of the evangelical counsels make a complete holocaust of man. Man has three sorts of goods: the goods of fortune,

---

* St. Th., 2, 2, q. 186, a. 7.

which he devotes to God by the vow of poverty; the goods of the body, which he offers up by the vow of chastity; and the goods of the soul, that are given to God by the vow of obedience.* When man has thus consecrated himself with all that he is and has to God, then it is that he truly becomes a religious.

To be a religious is to perform acts that are a worship of God. Now, sacrifice holds the chief place among such acts, and the most perfect sacrifice is the holocaust, whereby not only a part, but the whole victim, is offered to God. When, therefore, by the three vows of the evangelical counsels, man makes a holocaust of himself, he has performed the grandest act of religion, and he deserves to be called a religious in the highest sense of the name.† No Catholic can deny what we are taught in the school of St. Thomas and Suarez on the perfection of the end and means of the religious state; for, to put the secular life on the same footing as the religious would be to revive the error of Vigilantius.‡ The teaching of these great masters is the noblest apology of the religious life.

In defence of this divine institution unbelievers and worldlings have been told that as, according to their own principles, every one is free to live as he pleases, they ought not to complain of men

---

* St. Th., 2, 2, q. 186, a. 7.   † Id., opusc. 18, c. xi, et opusc. 19, c. i.
‡ *Nisi quis secundum Vigilantium dicat, quod status sæcularis vitæ statui religionis æquetur.* (Id., opusc. 17, c. xii.)

using their liberty to choose the better part; that often the misfortunes and deceptions of the world lead unhappy persons to despair and suicide, who in a cloister would have found peace for the present and hope for the future. Assuredly these statements are true; but there is more than that to be said in behalf of the religious life. Those who accused religious of leading an idle life, and of being useless to society, received a ready answer from St. Bernard and the Angelical: "It is not without a purpose that we hide ourselves in cloisters and in forests. I think there is no one among us who, if he did in the world the quarter of what he does here, would not be venerated as a saint, or pass for an angel. Yet he is daily reproached for the uselessness of his life." *

And to confirm the truth of these words, apologists have had only to show the religious state in the course of Christian ages, and even at the present day, forming the fairest ornament, as well as the greatest strength, of the Church; giving to God the glory which so many men refuse him; appeasing his wrath by the fervor of prayer, the heroism of penance, and the purity of a holy life; shielding against heresy the rights and doctrines of the Church; strengthening Catholics in the faith; defying every danger, to carry the light of the Gospel to nations buried in the darkness

---

* St. Th., *De erudit. princip.*, lib. 5, c. lxiii.

of unbelief; presenting to every one the spectacle of the grandest virtues; instructing the ignorant; in its solitude, saving science and letters that once had no other refuge; keeping for ages to come the precious books delivered by antiquity, ransoming from barbarians the enslaved and manacled captive; raising these monuments that are the masterpieces of Christian art, and which modern genius has not been able to rival; opening hospitable asylums to every misfortune and every suffering; visiting the sick; providing for the poor; clearing the forest; draining marshes; fertilizing the most arid deserts,—and all that, at the cost of sacrifices which the world does not even know how to admire.

By such fruits the tree can be known. No serious mind will be deceived, even though on so fertile a tree there should be some twigs that bear no fruit—some dry and worm-eaten branches.

But to the enlightened and sincere Catholic nothing can, it seems to us, give a grander and more correct notion of the religious state than what we have said on the perfection of its end and its means, and consequently of its superiority to the common Christian life.

CHAPTER IV.

ADVANTAGES OF THE RELIGIOUS STATE.

Because the religious state, in addition to the observance of the commandments, requires also the keeping of the counsels, one might be exposed to the delusion of believing that salvation is in that state more difficult and less secure, on account of the new obligations which have to be assumed. But Suarez takes upon himself to put this prejudice to the rout. The addition of a countermure to the walls of a fort, even though increasing the bulk of the building, protects it none the less. This is just what the state of perfection does when to the commandments it superadds the obligation of the counsels. First of all, there are in that state fewer occasions for violating God's law.* This would be the place to speak of the dangers of the world. The holy doctors of the Church have done so with their habitual vigorous logic and commanding eloquence. We shall limit ourselves to a few short quotations from them. Let us hearken, first, to the grand voice of St. Chrysostom: " Do

---

* Suar., *De statu perfectionis*, lib. 1, c. ii, n. 9.

not believe," says he, "that the state of the world is better than that of a city ruled over by a ferocious tyrant: it is still worse than that. It is no man, but the devil himself, that tyrannizes over all the earth, letting loose everywhere his destructive hordes. I see him stationed in a citadel overlooking the world; he issues his impious orders, and everywhere spreads corruption and anarchy. Worst of all, he separates the soul of man from her God. What tyranny, what captivity, what slavery, what war, what shipwreck, what famine, would not be preferable to such evils!"* Then addressing worldlings, whose example and language stifle virtue, he continues: "You do not content yourselves with extolling maxims in opposition to those of Jesus Christ, you furthermore bestow on vice attractive names. Thus, for instance, frequenting theatres is fashion; enriching one's self by every kind of means is to secure independence; desire of glory is greatness of soul; insolence is frankness; extravagance is charity; injustice is courage. After that you travesty virtue, by presenting it under names that make it ridiculous. You call rusticity temperance, imbecility justice, frugality meanness; and, what is most frightful, to your words you add the teaching of example."†

"The atmosphere of the world is poisonous for the soul," says St. Liguori. "The ways of society,

---

* *Adv. oppugnator. vitæ monast.*, lib. I, c. vii. † Ibid., lib. 3, c. vii.

bad example, bad language, are so many baits that attract us to earth, and draw us away from God. Every one is aware that dangerous occasions are the ordinary cause of the ruin of souls." *

It is indeed true that, with the grace of God, we may sanctify ourselves everywhere, just as, in the holiest places, we may fall under the weight of our weakness and the malice of the devil; but the same St. Liguori tells us that the souls lost in the world are many in number, while but few come to eternal ruin in religion. † St. Mary Magdalen of Pazzi, continues St. Liguori, used often to kiss the walls of her convent, exclaiming: "O walls, sacred walls, that shield me against the temptations of hell!" Whenever the saintly Mary Orsini saw a nun laugh, "Laugh," she would say,—"laugh, sister: you have reason to laugh. You are sheltered from the storms of the world." ‡

Not only the religious state delivers from the greater part of the occasions of sin which are so numerous in the world, but it also preserves man from transgressing the commandments, in obliging him to practise the counsels. The counsels of a wise friend, says the Angelical, are a great benefit, according to the words of the book of Proverbs, c. xxvii, 9: "Ointment and perfume

---

* "The Nun Sanctified," c. ii, n. 6.   † "Spiritual Letters."
‡ "The Nun Sanctified," ibid.

rejoice the heart, and the good counsels of a friend are sweet to the soul." Now, there is no friend or wise man above Christ: his counsels are, therefore, of the very highest utility. The evangelical counsels, he adds, are in themselves profitable to all. From want, however, of dispositions in persons not inclined to follow them, it happens at times that they are not an advantage to this or that person in particular.* But here is, according to Suarez, one of the great benefits of the counsels: they surround and protect the commandments. Where the counsels are violated, the commandments are in greater danger of being treated in the same way.† And, indeed, who does not see that he who gives up his own property is less exposed than another to seek riches by unjust means; and to allow himself to be carried away " into many unprofitable and hurtful desires " of the things of the earth, which, as the apostle says, " drown men into destruction and perdition"? (1 Tim. vi, 9.)

Again the state of perfection, and therefore the religious state, makes a holy life more easy, for two reasons, which Suarez sets forth. The first reason is: what renders a holy life easy is, above all, the habit of performing virtuous acts. Now, the state of perfection requires, and in itself entails, the frequent use of such acts, and the constant surmounting of the difficulties to be met

---

* Suar., lib. I, c. xi, n. 11. † Suar., lib. I, c. xi, n. 11.

with in the path of virtue. By its very nature, therefore, this state is of immense assistance for the acquirement, sustenance and increase of God's grace and the rights of heaven. Finally, there are in this state more means for the practice of virtue."* This is the second reason in support of our proposition. We shall confine ourselves to a bare enumeration of these larger means, for our scope is not exhortation, but instruction.

"Persons living in the world," says St. Liguori, "are trees planted in a parched soil, on which the dews of heaven rarely fall. Poor worldlings! you would wish to give much time to prayer and meditation, often to hear the word of God, and enjoy a little solitude and recollection. But your domestic cares, your parents, social exigencies, visits, and many other distractions, prevent you. On the other hand, religious are privileged trees, growing in a rich soil that is always watered by the showers of heaven. The Lord incessantly helps his spouses by the lights and inspirations of meditation, by sermons, spiritual books, and the good example of their companions. When we sin in the world, there is no one to warn or reprove us; but when one falls in the monastic state, his companions hurry to raise him up."† To these words of the holy doctor let us add that the frequent reception of the sacraments, constant direction, the watchfulness of superiors,

---

* Suar., lib. I, c. ii, n. 10.   † "The Nun Sanctified," c. ii, 7, 10.

the rule of a religious house which fills up the day with useful and holy occupations, present extraordinary resources for good, and often afford unspeakable consolation. This is also St. Liguori's opinion: "Look," says he, "among the great ladies of the world, and see whether there is one as happy as that humble religious, who, divested of all earthly bonds, seeks only to merit the approbation of God. Saint Scholastica was in the habit of saying that, if men knew how peaceful religious are in their houses, the whole world would become a solitude; people would scale the walls of convents, and renounce the goods of this earth, as St. Mary Magdalen of Pazzi used also to say." *

And this peace of fervent souls is not troubled by the commotions and storms of the political world. These souls are aware that God has special watchfulness over them. History informs us that, among the multitude of virgins who suffered death in the persecutions of the first ages of the Church, God did not allow a single one to be outraged: † which is certainly a great miracle. For, as Tertullian remarks, the tyrants of those days, in order more cruelly to torture Christian women, aimed at their chastity more than their lives, knowing well that they had greater fear of dishonor than of death. ‡ "Sacred virgins!"

---

* St. Lig., "The Nun Sanctified," c. ii, nn. 13, 16.
† Corn. à Lapide in 1. Cor. vii, 35.   ‡ Tertull., *De pudicitia*, c. i

cried out St. Ambrose, "there is a special assistance from heaven for you, who by chastity keep in spotless purity the nuptial couch of the Lord. What wonder that angels combat for you, since you vie with them in virtue!"*

Did not Jesus Christ give the counsel about abandoning all things to follow him only a few years before the fury of Jew and Gentile burst upon his first followers? Persecution, after all, can only make martyrs; and if, on embracing the religious state, one can entertain a fuller hope of dying for Christ, it is a still greater advantage. Hence, when a person has determined to enter the religious state, no account is to be taken of possible or even probable revolutions. They who aspire to that state are no better than those who have embraced it: why, then, would they fear to run the risk of the same dangers in order to merit a similar reward?

St. Liguori, after speaking of the pure joy of the religious life, remarks very sensibly that in it one is not out of the reach of the sufferings that are inseparable from life in this world; still, according to the same doctor, sorrows are there only for unfaithful souls. For fervent religious, the tribulations of their life are sweet consolations. Besides, it is ever true to say that religious receive the hundred-fold during their life. The holy doctor adds, that in the religious state one

---

* *De virgin.*, lib. I, c. viii.

dies with greater confidence; and that the soul of the religious is sooner purified after death. Indeed, the religious life is one of the most efficacious satisfactions for the sins that preceded it; and if, at the hour of death, the religious has some atonement to make, the Masses offered for him, and the prayers of his brethren, will shorten the time appointed for his purgatory. Finally, the religious, if faithful, will possess everlasting life. St. Bernard says that it is easy to pass from a cell to heaven. And St. Lawrence Justinian was wont to say that religion is the gate of heaven; for, to be a religious is a sign that one is already chosen to be a companion of the elect. St. Chrysostom wrote in these words to a monk: "God cannot lie; he has promised eternal life to whoso gives up the world. You have left everything: who, then, hinders you from reckoning with confidence on this promise?"*

---

* St. Lig., "The Nun Sanctified," c. ii, *passim.*

CHAPTER V.

IS THE RELIGIOUS STATE OBLIGATORY.

Though the advantages of the religious life are very great, we must not, however, conclude therefrom that the state in itself is obligatory. "If we consider the religious life in itself," says Suarez, "no one is by strict commandment bound to embrace or profess it." By itself a counsel entails no obligation, not even under pain of venial sin. This appears to me certain and clearly taught by the fathers whom I have quoted. For they say that works of counsel are altogether free, and may be omitted without any fault. Furthermore, St. Paul seems to teach the same thing clearly: "If a virgin marries, she does not sin: he who gives his daughter in marriage, does well," even when acting against a counsel. But no one says of a person sinning in light matters, that he does well, or does not commit any sin. The same can be applied to the other counsels as to that on virginity.

It is for this reason that Scripture does not blame persons who do not follow the counsels.

Indeed, a counsel of God manifested outwardly, or proposed to men, indicates only a judgment of God, approving what he counsels as being more useful and suitable to reach everlasting happiness with greater ease and perfection. And any mind that would array itself in opposition to a divine counsel, by holding such a counsel not to be a better and more useful means for salvation, would put a grievous affront on God, in thinking so ill of his counsels. But unwillingness to follow or observe a divine counsel, not because it is not considered very good, but because the will, for other motives, feels no leaning toward it, is no offence whatever to Jesus Christ.* Although the state of perfection is a profitable means for the acquirement of perfection, it is not, however, a necessary means. † Still, as Suarez observes, there are cases in which circumstances render the state of perfection obligatory. Thus, for instance, he who has taken a vow to enter religion is bound to keep his vow. ‡ There are also weak souls that find everywhere in the world proximate occasions for offending God mortally, and for whom religion would be a secure haven against tempests, an escape after spiritual shipwreck. In reference to this matter, we read as follows in St. Liguori:—

"If one thought that, by remaining in the

---

* Suar., lib. I, c. ix, n. 24.   † Suar., lib. I, c. v, n. 2.
‡ *Ex accidenti contingit ut aliquis ex necessitate talem statum assumat ut ex voto religionis.* (Suar., lib. I, c. xi, n. 13.)

world, he would lose his soul, either because he has experience of his weakness amid the dangers of the world, or because he does not find there the assistance that the religious state offers, he could not be excused from grievous sin were he to remain in the world, since he thereby would put himself in serious danger of losing his soul." Quoting then the words of another theologian, the holy doctor says: "If your conscience tells you—and it is often the case—that you will be abandoned by God, unless you follow his divine call; that you will be lost, unless you leave the world, etc., it would then be a sin for you not to accept the impulse of grace." "It does not appear doubtful," continues the same saint, "that they very much expose their salvation who, being certain of a call from God to the religious state, seek to persuade themselves that, by remaining in, or going back to, the world, they will be able to save themselves as easily as in religion." And he adds: "I do not wish to give any absolute decision on this subject, but let us earnestly pray to God to save us from the danger of resisting a vocation. For history relates tragic and numberless misfortunes, which are only the carrying out of the threats made in Scripture against those who are unfaithful to the call of heaven." The holy doctor ends with the following words: "Those who are called, are bound to become religious, for God will refuse them in the world the assistance he had in store for them in religion ; and though with ordinary graces they may be saved in the world, as a fact, it will be difficult for them to attain salvation." *

---
* *Theol. Mor.*, lib. 4, c. i. *Dub.* 5, n. 78, *passim.*

CHAPTER VI.

IS THE RELIGIOUS STATE A COUNSEL.

"THE state of perfection," says Suarez, "is not of precept, but of counsel." * From what we have hitherto said, it can be clearly inferred that the religious state is in itself better, more perfect, and more advantageous, than the common Christian life: *melior et perfectior et utilior;* it is therefore absolutely a matter of counsel.† We conclude from this that the state may be desired, vowed, and counselled: *appeti et voveri et consuli potest.*‡ These are the words of Suarez: "The religious state not only is a state of perfection, but, furthermore, it is an excellent thing to desire it, to ask for it, to embrace it: *modus obtinendi illum, ipsum appetendo, petendo et procurando, optimus est.* Hence one acts all the more perfectly and prudently in embracing it, the more spontaneous and free his action is in so doing. It is quite another thing with respect to the cure of souls. The more we fear that burden the greater our security in taking it up, especially when we resign ourselves to it out of obedience to superiors."§

St. Thomas had said before Suarez: "It is

---

* Suar., lib. I., c. xi, n. 12. † Ibid., c. xxi, n. 5.
‡ Ibid , c. xviii, n. 11. § Ibid., lib. I, c. xxi, n. 5.

meritorious to desire the religious state. The religious state does not presuppose perfection, but leads to it; whereas the episcopal dignity presupposes it. To desire perfection and wish to attain it does not appear to be presumption, but a holy emulation to which the apostle exhorts us: 'Be zealous for the better gifts.' (1 Cor. xii, 31.) On this account it is praiseworthy to embrace the religious state, while it is too presuming to aspire to the honors of prelacy."* After a parallel between a king and a monk, and having shown how far happier is the lot of the latter than that of the mightiest monarch, St. John Chrysostom concludes in these eloquent words: "When you see a rich man passing, splendidly dressed, all ablaze with gold, and pompously drawn in a magnificent chariot, do not say, 'That man is happy.' Riches are only an apparent good, that is as transitory and fleeting as life itself. But, when you see passing a modest and recollected solitary with mild and kindly look, envy the lot of that man, imitate his wisdom, and long to resemble the just man. 'Ask,' says the Lord, 'and you shall receive.' These are the real goods,—the goods that save and last forever."†

From these words of the holy doctor, we can easily infer that it is good to beg of God a religious vocation. And if the religious state is the surest means of salvation for him who solicits the grace, God will certainly hear his prayer,

---

* Opusc. 18, c. xix.   † Migne, t. 1, col. 392.

provided it fails in none of the conditions which he requires. Has not our Lord promised to grant all we shall ask in his name? From what precedes, it follows, also, that a vow to not embrace or seek the religious state is in itself illicit and invalid, unless some special circumstances excuse it;* while it is in itself a very good thing to bind one's self by vow to enter religion.† This last proposition is certain and of faith, says Suarez: *certa de fide*. Since it is an act of virtue to enter religion, and more praiseworthy to practise an act of virtue under vow, they deserve praise who, not being able to enter religion, take a vow to do so.‡ Such is the reasoning of St. Thomas. "We consider here the vow in itself; for, to judge whether it is advantageous for this or that person in particular, circumstances must be taken into consideration; and, first, to take a vow of the kind, one must have the requisite age. There is an age required for its validity, and an age for its opportuneness. To take the vow validly, it is enough to have reached the age of reason, and to have employed on it as much deliberation as is necessary for a mortal sin. Though such a vow taken by a girl not yet twelve, or by a boy not yet fourteen, is valid, it has not, however, its full force; for it can be annulled by parents in case they did not ratify the vow after their daughter reached her twelfth, or their son his fourteenth, year.

---

* Suar., lib. 1, c. xxiii, n. 13. † Id., lib. 4, c. i, n. 2.
‡ St. Th., opusc. 17, c. xii.

"In order that the vow to enter religion should be opportune, it must be made at a proper age and with serious deliberation,—more serious, in fact, than for other vows or for temporal affairs. Children, therefore, should not be exhorted in a light way to make such a vow; for, as it is easy to induce them, so they change very readily. When consulted on the matter," says Suarez, from whom all we are here saying is taken, "if, after due reflection, we think the person asking counsel could to advantage enter the religious state, and is exposed to alter his mind unless he strengthens himself by a vow, we may very well encourage him to make the vow, not, indeed, by annoying requests, but by reasons drawn from faith."* St. Thomas is still more explicit than Suarez on this question.† He who has vowed to enter religion is bound to keep his vow. He must consequently take steps to obtain his admission into some religious house, and, if admitted, he should enter. This vow, even when taken in early youth, always binds, unless it has been annulled. If, when taking the vow, one determines in his mind and promises the time for carrying it out, he is obliged to enter religion at the time so determined; but, when he does not fix the precise date of this entrance, he is bound, however, to enter as soon as possible. Yet the fulfilment of this kind of a vow may for just reasons be

---

* Suar., lib. 4, c. i, n. 3. † Opusc. 17, c. xii.

deferred. Guilty negligence and voluntary delays do not remove the obligation. Therefore, even when the time for entering mentioned in the vow is passed, the one who made the vow remains bound to his engagement, unless—and this rarely occurs—he had, when making his vow, a formal intention to the contrary. Although a reasonable cause suffices for putting off the execution of such a vow, yet care is to be taken lest delays should bring on entire faithlessness, and we should fear the sins that may be committed in the world. A long delay, having no excuse in its favor, would be grievously sinful. He who vowed to enter religion, but has not succeeded in gaining admission, though he took all the necessary steps to secure it, is freed from the obligation of his vow, provided he has no hope of gaining admission at some future day.*

Vows to enter the religious state properly so called are reserved to the Sovereign Pontiff; that is, he alone has the power to dispense from them, or to change them. The vow to enter a society not approved of by the Church, is not reserved to the pope.† The same is true with respect to communities of women as now existing in France, except Savoy. ‡

---

*Suar., lib. 4, c. ii, n. 3; Gautrelet, *Traité de l'état religieux*; Liguori, *Theol. Mor.*, lib. 4, n. 72. †Suar., ibid., c. vii, n. 1.

‡ Gautrelet, *Traité de l'état religieux*, t. 1, p. 62; Gury, *Cas. Consc.*, t. 2, n. 98.

CHAPTER VII.

IS IT ALLOWABLE TO EXHORT PERSONS TO ENTER RELIGION.

ST. THOMAS puts himself this question, and returns the following answer: "Those who entice others to enter religion, not only commit no sin, but even merit a great reward. For it is written: 'He who causeth a sinner to be converted from the error of his way shall save his soul from death, and shall cover a multitude of sins' (James v, 20); and: 'They that instruct many to justice shall shine as stars for all eternity.' (Dan. xii, 3.)"*

Thus St. Thomas, as Suarez remarks, is of opinion that in itself it is good to induce persons, by true and solid reasons, to enter the religious state. And here is the ground of the holy doctor's teaching: "Entrance into religion is in itself a good act; and it is praiseworthy to induce persons to perform good acts."† Suarez recommends prudence in the matter; but acknowledges, meanwhile, that the truth is to be freely told to any one that seeks advice. "He," adds the same theologian, "whom the Holy Ghost begins to impel toward the religious life must be

---
* St. Th., 2, 2, q. 189, a. 9.   † Suar., lib. 5, c. viii, n. 10.

helped, so that he may remain steadfast in his purpose, or may not resist grace, and may more readily obtain, through prayer and good works, more abundant graces." This learned theologian, though considering that it is rarely proper to exhort a person directly to enter the religious state before the Holy Ghost has begun to call him, still recognizes and teaches that it is very good to excite all souls to purity of conscience, to fear the occasions of sin, and to lay before them at the same time the advantages and excellence of the religious state.* And, indeed, this is what our Lord himself did: "If thou wilt be perfect, go sell what thou hast, and give to the poor, and thou shalt have treasure in heaven. And every one that hath left house, or brethren, or sisters, or father, or mother, or wife, or children, or lands, for my name's sake, shall receive an hundred-fold, and shall possess life everlasting." (Matt. xix, 21, 29.)

In the three books in which he writes a defence of the monastic state, St. Chrysostom relates that already, in his own day, those who taught the religious life were subjected to severe persecution. The holy doctor takes up their defence with all his eloquence, and having made a most appalling description of the world of that time, he exclaims: "If we knew a place unhealthy and subject to pestilence, would we not withdraw our

---

* Suar., lib. 5, c. viii, n. 10.

children from it, without being stopped by the riches that might be heaped up in it, or by the fact that their health had not as yet suffered, and might, perhaps, be secure in it from all danger? And yet, now that so deadly a contagion has overspread everything, not only are we the first to push these same children into the chasm, but we even drive away as impostors those who would fain keep them back from destruction." *

Farther on, the saint adds: " Among seculars shipwrecks are more frequent and sudden, because the difficulties of navigation are greater; but with anchorites storms are less violent, the calm is almost undisturbed. This is the reason why we seek to draw as many as we can to the desert. We draw them to it, not merely to make them wear haircloth, but that they may shun evil and practise virtue."† What is there more forcible and more touching than the letter of St. Jerome to Heliodorus inciting him to quit the world? In it the saint begs, weeps, reproves, exhorts, and enters into poetical eulogies of solitude: " I invite you, make haste. You have made light of my entreaties; perhaps you will listen to my reproaches. Effeminate soldier! What are you doing under the paternal roof? Where are the palisade and the entrenchment? Where is the winter passed under tent? Even though your

---

* *Adv. oppugn. vit. monast.*, lib. 3, c. viii, ed. Migne, t. I, col. 362.
† Ibid., c. xv, ed. Migne, t. I, col. 375.

little nephew should twine around your neck; even were your mother with streaming hair to show you, through her rent garment, the breast that nurtured you; even if your father were to throw himself across the threshold of your house, step over the obstacle, and with unquivering eye rush to take your place under the standard of the cross. Our heart is not of iron, nor are our feelings dead; the tigress born amid the mountains of Hyrcania has not given us suck—still we have burst all our bonds. Lo, your sister, who has lost her husband, presses you in her arms; your attendants who have witnessed your growth, say to you, 'Whom shall we henceforth serve?' your nurse, your grandmother, your tutor, who, next to your father, has a claim on your filial affection, exclaim, 'Wait a while until we are dead; bury us before you go,'—love for God and fear of hell easily break all chains. O solitude, all spangled with the flowers of Jesus Christ! O solitude, wherein are shaped the stones that build up the city of the great King! Blessed retreat where one enjoys familiarity with God! Brother dear, what are you doing in the world, which is so far less than you? How long more shall the paternal roof shelter your head? Will you tarry much longer in the smoky prison of cities? Do you fear hardship? And what athlete was ever crowned without a struggle? It is my love for you, O brother! that has urged me to say these things, to the end that, on judgment-day, you may share the glory of those who now live amid the holy rigors of penance."*

St. Augustine also wrote: "I have been passionately fond of the perfection of the evangelical counsels: with God's grace I have embraced it. With all the power I have, I exhort others to do the same; and I have companions whom I have succeeded to persuade."†

But there is nothing more striking than the example of St. Bernard. The details are taken from the best historians of his admirable life.‡ This saint in the flower of his youth, at the age of twenty, began to feel the impulse of grace drawing to retirement from the busy world. He not only triumphed over the opposition of his family, but drew to his purpose his uncle and his brothers, and took with him to Citeaux thirty of the noblest gentlemen of his country. To increase the little flock that he had brought together, this incomparable young man was endowed with a marvellous and heavenly winningness of manner. Indeed, so attractive was he, that, whenever he preached, mothers concealed their sons, wives their husbands, and friends kept their friend out of Bernard's way.

Nor is it only in the later times of Christianity that the fathers and doctors of the Church have held up before generous souls the excellence and

---

* St. Hieron. ad Heliodor., *passim.*
† Epist. 157, ed. Migne, col. 692, ad Hilar., n. 39.
‡ Ed. Migne: *Inter opera S. Bern.*, t. 4, p. 656, et seqq.

advantages of the religious state. To be convinced of this, we have only to quote a letter of St. Liguori, the doctor of the Church, the missioner of consummate experience, the bishop of truly apostolic heart, who lived in the eighteenth century. Here is what he wrote, at the close of his long and laborious career, to one of his relatives. His letter bears date April 23, 1771: "I have not forgotten that, only a few years ago, you seemed desirous to form an alliance with Jesus Christ. I pray to the Lord to strengthen in you this holy disposition. In the world it would be difficult for you to keep yourself in the grace of God. What I say to you, I repeat to all young women who come to ask my advice. I always remind them that, such is the corruption of the world, they will meet in it a thousand hindrances to their salvation. You should then fear to abandon Christ for the world. Thus far I have had the consolation to see all my relatives whom death has snatched away, die a good death. I hope, one day, to be in their company in heaven, and to meet you there. Beg of God to grant me a happy death; for I feel that my last hour is not far distant."* This is sufficient to show the teaching and practice of the great doctors of the Church in reference to the subject on which we are now engaged. Their lessons have in all ages borne abundant fruit.

---

* "Spiritual Letters," ed. Perisse, 1834, let. 121.

The number of religious who, in the fourth century, lived in the solitudes of Egypt would be incredible, were it not supported by undeniable testimony. In our own times, notwithstanding the worldly prejudices amid which Christian souls have to live, in spite of the hatred manifested by thousands against the religious state, not only are ancient religious orders flourishing with renewed vigor, but around them are growing up many new and fair trees that shade and ornament the fertile fields of the Church.

Let those who may be alarmed at the multiplication of religious communities and the numbers who enter them, give ear to the following words of St. John Chrysostom, which one would almost suppose written for the days in which we live: " It is not the observance of the commandments and counsels of Jesus Christ that exposes society to danger. Who is it that troubles the world and upsets order? Is it those who lead a wise and regular life; or those who invent new and hitherto unheard-of means to flatter the passions? Are they men deeply interested in the welfare of all, or those who think only of what concerns themselves? Are they the lovers of obedience, or rather the place- and office-seekers who shrink from no daring or enterprise? Are they those who build for themselves sumptuous mansions, and feast at luxurious tables; or those who seek nothing beyond the bare necessaries of food and lodging? Are they those who employ every wicked artifice to achieve wealth; or they who subtract from their own to assist the indigence of others? Of these two classes of men, one is the scourge of society, and may be compared to tumors that destroy the beauty of the body; or to those furious winds that upheave the sea, and cause numberless shipwrecks. Is it not they who bring on revolutions, wars, and battles; the sacking of towns, the imprisonment and bondage of men, murders, and a thousand other evils of this life? Are not they the authors, not only of the evils that men cause men, but of those others which heaven pours on men—such as droughts, inundations, earthquakes, the ruin and swallowing up of cities, famine, pestilence, and all the chastisements which angry heaven heaps upon us? These are the men who overthrow states and destroy governments. It is for them that are established courts of justice, laws and penalties of sundry kinds. On the contrary, the other class, like lighthouses shining afar in the night, summon from every quarter, to secure and tranquil havens, the wretched seaman who is tossed about on the waters and in extreme danger of his life. Lighting up in high places the lamp of wisdom, they lead, as it were, by the hand, men of good-will to the port of safety and peace."*

---

* St. Chrysost., *adv. oppugn. vit. monast.*, lib. 3, c. ix, ed Migne, vol. 1, coll. 363, 364.

CHAPTER VIII.

FAULTS TO BE SHUNNED WHILE INDUCING PERSONS TO EMBRACE THE RELIGIOUS LIFE.

ACCORDING to Suarez, these faults may all be ranged under the three heads mentioned by St. Thomas, namely, violence, simony, and fraud.*

When the French Revolution, under pretence of restoring captives to liberty, broke open the gates and grates of convents, it met in these holy retreats souls that would have preferred death to the liberty which was offered to them. Nothing short of sacrilegious violence could have dragged these religious from the abodes that sheltered them from the dangers of the world; for the Church displays wondrous wisdom in her institutions, and, next to God, no one shows greater respect than she does for the freedom of man. "It would," says the Angelical, "be exceedingly wrong to force any one into religion; and Pope Nicholas I forbids it to be done."†

Violence when great, and such as would make impression on a courageous man, annuls the

---
* Suar., lib. 5, c. viii, n. 10; St. Th., 2, 2, q. 189, a. 9.   † Ibid.

religious profession. It implies grave injustice, as Suarez observes.* The Church sought, above all, to protect the freedom of women, whose weakness has need of greater support. For this reason the Council of Trent excommunicates those who, by violence or fear, compel a woman to enter religion.† Also bishops in person, or, if prevented, by delegates, are bound to ascertain the freedom of young women who embrace the religious life; and bishops must do this, first, at the clothing, and secondly, before the novices take the vows.‡

The second fault to be feared when exhorting others to embrace the religious life is, according to St. Thomas, simony. This name is given to the crime which he would commit who, with money, would attempt to purchase the entrance of any one into religion: and this also is forbidden by the laws of the Church. The holy doctor observes, however, that it would not be wrong to assist a poor person, so that he or she might be able to become a religious; and he adds that it is also allowed to give some little presents without agreement, so as to conciliate the good-will of another, and bring him afterward more efficaciously to understand what will be said to him with respect to the advantages of a religious life.§

Lastly, the third defect would be to induce a person to become a religious through lies. There

---

* Suar., lib. 5. c. ix. n. 1.   † Ibid., 2.
‡ Lig., lib. 4, n. 5.   § St. Th., 2, 2, q. 189, a. 9.

would be reason to fear that he about whom such means would have been used, finding himself deceived, might return to the world, and thus render his last state worse than his first.*

But now, supposing these three defects, which we have just pointed out, to be avoided,—and in our times they are very rare, not to say unheard of,—the general rule remains such as the Angelical Doctor laid it down: "Those who entice others to enter religion not only do not sin, but, furthermore, merit a great reward." Parents, therefore, deserve a great recompense who train up their children for God, and whose most ardent desire is to see those same children consecrate themselves to God. This was the noble ambition of Aleth, the mother of St. Bernard. As an ancient historian relates, she had seven children, who were born rather for the monastery of Citeaux, than for their own family. As long as their mother lived she brought them up less for the court than the cloister, always keeping them from delicacies, and giving them only plain food. She had a special affection for Bernard, whose future greatness had been revealed to her in a dream from heaven. As soon as he was born she consecrated him to God, not merely as she had done with her other children, but in a special way setting him apart, and vowing him to the service of God. But Bernard soon lost his

---

* St. Th., 2, 2, q. 189, a. 9.

virtuous mother; so that, when his brothers made every effort to dissuade him from following the religious life, he felt his resolution shaken. Yet the thought of that mother constantly haunted him; everywhere her sweet face met him, and seemed to say to him: "Is it for the vanities of the world, my son, that I brought you up with such care?" This thought confirmed him in his purpose to quit the world.* Thank heaven! the ideas of this noble woman have not yet died out in the minds of men. At the present day there are still parents sufficiently enlightened to understand that the greatest bliss of their children is to give themselves to God, and generous enough to sacrifice with joy to the Lord all that they hold to be most precious in this life. Especially there are mothers, who, yearning for what the world fears, constantly ask of God a religious vocation for their children: and they do this, not with human views, but from motives of the purest faith. Blessed parents! the everlasting happiness which they will enjoy with their children in heaven, will be the reward of their liberality to God.

From all this we are to conclude, once more, that, to speak the language of St. Thomas, those friends act in a praiseworthy manner—*laudabiliter facere*—who give their friends a relish for the loveliness and consolations of the religious state.

---

* *Inter opera S. Bern.*, ed. Migne, tom. 4, p. 553, et seqq.

And the great recompense of which the Angelic Doctor speaks, will be given also to priests and pastors of souls who, within the bounds of prudence, which is to be their constant guide, shall employ the means presented to them by their holy ministry to make the religious state admired, sought after, and beloved. They will be condemned and criticised bitterly by those only who fall in with the prejudices of the world, and understand nothing about evangelical perfection.

But some may inquire: "Is there not reason to fear lest, in holding up the religious life to souls, we should lead persons to embrace it who are not called by God?" Remember, says St. Thomas, that if entrance into religion, whereby a soul gets near to Christ and seeks to follow him, is suggested by the devil or by any human being, such suggestion has no weight, unless the one to whom it is made be called by God. The desire to enter religion always originates with God, no matter who inspires it.* They likewise do well who, by their exhortations, urge others to that state, thereby coöperating in the action of the Holy Ghost, and endeavoring to enforce by exterior influence what he impels to by his interior working. Are we not the helpers of God, as St. Paul expresses it? (1 Cor. iii, 9.)† Still, when speaking to the faithful of the hundred-fold promised by our Lord to those who leave all to follow him,

---

* St. Th., opusc. 17, c. x. † Ibid., c. xii.

it is good to bring to their notice this other remarkable saying of the divine teacher: "If any one wishes to come after me, let him deny himself, and take up his cross and follow me." (Matt. xvi, 24.) The religious state grants the consolations of grace to those only who sacrifice the tendencies of nature. Indeed, with God's help, abnegation becomes easy for generous souls. "Take up my yoke upon you... and you shall find rest for your souls. For my yoke is sweet, and my burden light." (Matt. xi, 29, 30.)

CHAPTER IX.

OPPOSITION TO THE RELIGIOUS LIFE.

Having anathematized those who oblige women to enter religion, the holy Council of Trent also subjects to a like anathema those "who shall, in any way, without a just cause, hinder the holy wish of virgins or other women to take the veil, or make their vows."* This excommunication was incurred by the employment of fraud or violence, not by promises or entreaties.† The penalty would not fall on persons dissuading from entering a religious congregation, because the legislator had in view only properly called religious orders.‡

But this wise rigor of the Church shows very well that it is criminal to throw unjust obstacles in the way of religious vocations. "I am of opinion," says Suarez, "that he who deceives another in order to turn him away from the religious life, sins mortally. He commits a grave injustice in reference to the one he deceives, and sometimes in reference also to the community from

---

* *Conc. Trid.*, sess. 25, c. xviii.   † Suar., lib. 5, c. ix, nn. 13, 14.
‡ Gautrelet, t. 1, p. 52.

which he keeps the person. Fraud is in itself bad and hurtful to the neighbor, particularly when there is question of giving counsels. And, indeed, he who undertakes the office of counsellor, by the very fact binds himself, by a species of tacit contract, to give sincere counsel; and this obligation grows weightier when the counsel given has reference to morals, and when deceit leads the neighbor to great losses. Now, all this takes place in the point under consideration. I do not hesitate to say that in such a matter fraud involves serious injustice. The religious state is not, indeed, necessary for salvation, still that does not change the question; nor does it hinder him who is deprived of it against his will by unlawful means, from suffering great harm. This or that office or benefice is not necessary for salvation, nor even at times for this present life; and yet there is no doubt that it is a heinous injustice fraudulently to hinder another from obtaining such office or benefice. With much more reason, then, is this doctrine true when similar means are employed to turn a person away from the religious state." * And this sin, already grievous in itself, may become still more so, if, for instance, in order to keep one fraudulently from religion, a person were to heinously slander the religious life in general, or some order in particular. This sin is committed, not only by deceiving him who

---

* Suar., lib. 5, c. ix, n. 8.

seeks counsel, but also when of our own accord we take upon ourselves to give bad advice to others, to deceive them and thus stifle their holy intentions. For the malice of this sin does not principally consist in making an ill use of the office of adviser, though this circumstance also increases the sin in no small degree, but it consists rather in a fraud that entails much harm for our neighbor.*

But what are we to think of those who, seeking without just reason, to divert others from embracing the religious life, employ, not violence or falsehood, but mere promises and entreaties? St. Liguori will inform us. Here is what we read in his work called "Practice of Confession:" "If the intention of him who desires to become a religious is good, and if he is under no impediment, neither the confessor nor any one else can, as St. Thomas teaches, without grievous sin, hinder or divert a penitent from following that calling, though prudence may sometimes counsel delay in the execution of the purpose, in order better to test the firmness and perseverance of the aspirant in his resolution."† It is clear that this sin, which is grievous for all, would be still more so for those who have charge of souls, and who, for that very reason, are bound by their office to promote the spiritual progress of souls. The same inference will appear in greater

---

* Suar., lib. 5, c. ix, n. 9.   † *Praxis confess.*, c. vii, n. 92.

evidence from the following passage which we extract from the larger work of the saint on Moral Theology. Having said that no one excuses from grievous sin parents who, by threats, violence, or fraud, unjustly dissuade their children from entering the religious state, the holy bishop continues: " We must at all events admit, for it is the common teaching of theologians, that those parents sin mortally who turn away their children from the religious life, whether by fraud and violence, by entreaties, promises, or in any other manner." The saint then cites twenty theologians who hold this view, and goes on: " Many of these authors look upon as guilty of grievous sin, not parents only, but even strangers, who divert others from the religious life. My view is, that parents in this case are guilty of another sin against the duty of their state; for they are bound, under pain of grievous sin, to promote the spiritual advancement of their children."* Hence God sometimes chastises in this life this sinful opposition to his purposes. " Many young men," says St. Liguori again, " have lost their vocation through the fault of their parents; and not only have they come themselves to a bad end, but they have brought ruin on their families. A young man, influenced by his father, was unfaithful to his religious vocation; later he had violent quarrels with his father, in one of which

---

* " Practice of Love for Christ," c. xi, n. 14.

he killed him, and afterward met death himself on a scaffold. How many equally tragic examples could we not cite? However, I do not say that many parents, at least where their opposition is of short duration, may not be free from mortal sin on account of their ignorance or inadvertence. Their excessive natural love for their children may easily keep their duty out of sight."* But how can ignorance excuse before God those who are acquainted with the teachings of theology on this subject? Here the remark of Lessius naturally finds its place. Speaking of parents who disinherit their children that wish to enter religion, and oblige them to give up their legitimate rights, he says: "Such action is illicit and unjust, whether we consider the counsels of Jesus Christ and the divine right which follows from them, or whether we view the civil law, the canon law, the teaching of the fathers of the Church, and the reasons that condemn so odious a practice."†

Already, in the fourth century, St. Ambrose complained bitterly that mothers, and, what is still worse, widowed mothers, feared to see in their daughters zeal for virginity vowed to God. "If your daughters," said he, "wished to love a man, the law would allow them to choose the one most acceptable to them: and will it not then be allowed them who can choose a man to choose

---

* *Theol. Mor.*, lib. 4, n. 77. † Lessius, q. xi, at the beginning.

a God?"* Then addressing the children of these women, the holy doctor exhorts them not to entertain too great a fear of being disinherited by their parents: "They will refuse you a dower, but your spouse is rich; and rejoicing in his treasures, you can readily forego a paternal inheritance. Is not poverty, when combined with chastity, above all the dowers of earth? Besides, have you ever heard that love of virtue ever caused a young woman to be disinherited? Your parents, indeed, oppose you, but they are willing to be worsted in the contest. They resist your holy desires, which they are afraid to believe in; they often grow indignant with you, that you may learn to overcome all obstacles to your purpose."† Frequently, indeed, the threats of parents are barren of results; and the same parents end by greater fondness for those very children who, in spite of them, have devoted their lives to God. St. John Chrysostom will soon give us evidence of this fact. Indeed, parents would incur no guilt if they opposed the vocation of their children for just reasons: as, for instance, in a case where their entrance into religion would leave parents in great destitution, or expose a family of high social position to extinction. "However, I am of opinion," says St. Liguori, "that in this latter case a child would not be bound for such a motive to renounce his

---

* *De virginitate*, lib. I, c. x, ed. Migne.   † Ibid., c. xi.

vocation."* Here we see that the law of God and the teaching of the saints respect the rights of parents as well as those of children, and protect the interests of both with equal care.

St. Chrysostom has written admirable pages of exhortation to parents, in order to induce them to sacrifice generously to God even their only child in case he should call for it. With vehement logic he proves to them that in the cloister their children will be more truly rich, more esteemed, less liable to sickness, more powerful, and freer, than they could be in the world.† He also adds that in the religious life they will feel greater respect for their parents. "The religious," says he, "who is so good and gentle to all, will not be wanting in the tenderest veneration for his father. Had he been raised to some high office in the world, who knows whether he would not have despised that same father? But in the career which he has chosen,—a career that raises him above kings, he will be in his parents' presence the most dutiful of children. In the world, perhaps, he would have coveted riches, and for that reason would have been anxious for you to die; now, on the contrary, he begs of God that your life may be prolonged for many years. Had he even to lay down his own life to save yours, he would not refuse the sacrifice; for he serves and

---

* *Theol. Moral.*, lib. 3, n. 335.
† *Adv. oppugnat. vit. monast.*, lib. 2, *passim.*

obeys you, not from the law of nature alone, but, above all, out of obedience to God, for whose sake he has trampled on every earthly advantage. Why, then, I ask, do you complain? Is it because you have not to fear lest that son should on any day fall in battle, or because he is not at the mercy of envious companions? As persons who have put a young child in some elevated position are in constant dread lest he should fall, so those parents have little peace of mind whose son has been raised to a high place in the world.

"But have not the sword and the military uniform some charm? Yes; but how long will that last—a hundred, two hundred days? And, after that, does not every thing seem like a dream? You wished to see your son nobly attired, mounted on a splendid charger, and followed by a crowd of attendants? Why were you eager for that? Was it to procure him pleasure? Well, then, were you to hear him assert that he considers his life happier than that of men who enjoy every delight, and that he would rather die than forego his present happiness,—what would you say? Do you not know the joys of a life exempt from care?"* "No, your son's present lot does not call for tears. He deserves to be covered with applause for having made choice of a life free from turmoil, for having taken refuge

---

* *Adv. oppugnat. vit. monast.*, lib. 2, c. ix.

in a port so secure. But you will be exposed to the reproaches of many parents whose sons are settled in the world; for, in seeing you sacrifice your son, some will go into tears, and others will rail at you. And why are you not the first to make light of them, and to mourn over the blindness of such people? Ah! let us not look whether people turn us into mockery, but whether they do so with reason. If we deserve their gibes, we ought to weep before they say anything to us; but if we do not, let us congratulate ourselves, and pity the silly persons who seek to make us ridiculous. It is only fools that jeer at what is praiseworthy. I had a friend whose unbelieving father was wealthy, esteemed, and distinguished in every way. This father first had recourse to the magistrates, then he threatened his son with prison, stripped him of all he possessed, and sent him to a distant country, without allowing him even the barest necessaries for the support of life. The object of all this harshness was to force his son to return to the world. But when the father saw that the young man was proof against all this ill-treatment, he entirely changed his conduct toward him, and to-day he venerates his child as he would a parent. This happy father is indebted to that son for still greater honor than he had hitherto enjoyed in the world."*

---

* *Adv. oppugnat. vit. monast.*, lib. 2, c. x.

"You are well pleased that your children remain with you to serve and help you," continues St. John Chrysostom, from whom we borrow this lengthy passage. "I in turn desire as ardently as you, their father, that they should make a fitting return to you for the care which you took in bringing them up. However, to have them taught human learning, you send them far away from their native land, and forbid the paternal roof to those who go to learn a mere trade, or something still less honorable. Will you not, then, allow those to leave your house who want to learn how to fly from earth to heaven? You have courage enough to put up with any absence of your children, no matter how protracted, if it will only redound to their temporal welfare. Well, when they absent themselves in the interest of their souls, is it reasonable in you to be so far weak and tender as to blast by your pusillanimity the fairest hopes of the very highest fortune?

"After all you can visit frequently your children who are religious: and this you cannot do with others of them who are making long journeys. Who hinders you from going to the religious houses where your children dwell, and calling on them, since they cannot come to you? There you can talk with them on the important question of salvation. These visits will assuredly not end in the barren and unprofitable joy of a mere sight of them, or a talk with them. You will withdraw from the monastery to your homes better than you went to them, and you will take back with you the precious fruits of a holy and charming conversation." *

---

* *Adv. oppugnat. vit. monast.*, lib. 3, c. xviii.

CHAPTER X.

HINDRANCES TO THE RELIGIOUS LIFE.

WHILE admiring the religious state, and condemning those who turn others away from it, Catholic doctrine confesses that in certain cases there are serious reasons to retain in the world some persons who would wish to leave it. Theologians make mention of hindrances to entering the religious state: we, too, shall say a few words upon them. Girls under twelve, and boys under fourteen, cannot, without the consent of their parents or guardians, become religious. Any one for whom marriage is in given cases obligatory, cannot enter religion. The cases in which marriage is obligatory are rare, and we have already spoken of them in Art. I, Chapter II, of this book. No bishop can become a religious without the permission of the pope. Except in a few rare cases, married persons are not free to enter religion without the consent of husband or wife, as the case may be.* The entrance of the religious state is forbidden by the Sovereign Pontiffs to debtors who have lost their property

---

* St. Lig., *Theol. Mor.*, lib. 4, n. 65.

through their own fault, and are exposed to lawsuits with their creditors. This prohibition does not concern such as can pay their liabilities at the same time that they retire from the world.*

It is not right to enter a convent when one knows well that he is unable to bear its burdens and obligations: as, for instance, when one has a latent disease, or some infirmity of body or of mind, that is incompatible with the work and perfection of a religious life. In such a case it would be a sin to hide these impediments. But if the applicant makes known his condition, and is accepted notwithstanding his defects, he may enter without any sin, in the hope that no more will be required of him than he can perform.†

Parents who have children under age cannot leave the world, unless they previously make provision for these children. When, however, their children are of age, the parents are not bound to remain with them, unless their children are in extreme need of their assistance.‡

But can children enter religion and leave their parents in want? Before answering this question, we must state that there are various degrees of want. There is extreme, great, and common want. Extreme want is that of a man who is exposed to die unless some one helps him. Great want is that of one who finds it very difficult to live, who

---

* St. Lig., *Theol. Mor.*, lib. 4, n. 71.
† Suar., lib. 5, c. iv, n. 19.   ‡ Ibid., lib. 4, n. 69.

is in misery, has to lower himself so as to fall considerably below his rank; or, again, has to beg for a living, to follow a trade altogether below his former state of life. Common want is that in which those persons live who, by work and economy, can get what is necessary to support themselves, yet have to be very sparing, and to deprive themselves, not only of superfluities, but at times even of what would be useful.*

When parents are in extreme want, children cannot abandon them to enter religion. The same is true of brothers and sisters.†

A person may defer leaving the world, or even remain in it altogether, with a view to help his brothers who are in great want; yet, in a case of this nature, there is no obligation to give up a vocation. ‡ Parents that are in great want must not be abandoned, according to the teaching of St. Thomas and St. Liguori, and the common opinion of theologians. Suarez does not think that this obligation extends to grand-parents: *neque etiam ad avos.* § Yet, in order that in this case a child should be obliged to remain in the world, there must first be a hope that, by so remaining, he will be able to assist his parents; for, if he were to be of no help to them, he would not be held to forego the religious life. Secondly, there must be no other children to assist the

---

* Suar., lib. 5, c. v, n. 2. † St. Lig., *Theol. Mor.*, lib. 4, nn. 66 et 70.
‡ Ibid., n. 70. § Suar., ibid., n. 9.

parents.* Finally, if, by remaining in the world, a child were exposed to the danger of sinning grievously, and he could not remove that danger, he would be allowed to enter religion, no matter what might be the wants of his parents; because the eternal salvation of the child must take precedence of the temporal life of his parents.†

Suarez goes still further: "A father," says he, "cannot force his child, who lives with him in order to help him, to omit works of perfection that are not incompatible with the service which he requires from him. To oblige a child to give up such works would be a great loss to him, and would be exacting from him that to which the father has no right. Were, then, his father to employ force to prevent the child from practising works of perfection, such, for instance, as perpetual chastity; or if he urged him by direct provocation to desist from such works, the child would have sufficient reason to shun his father's presence, and even to leave him entirely, were such a step necessary in order to shelter himself from these assaults."‡

A child is never bound to renounce the religious state to help his parents, who, on account of his separation from them, might have to bear some privations, but yet would not be reduced to misery or loss of rank in society. Do not

---

* Suar. lib. 5, c. v, n. 4.   † St. Lig., *Theol. Mor.*, lib. 4, n. 66.
‡ Ibid., n. 29.

parents every day make immense sacrifices to set their children up in the world? They would, therefore, be very much in the wrong, if they refused to make a sacrifice when their children have a desire to embrace a state the most perfect and the most advantageous for their salvation. For this reason all theologians exempt from sin children who leave their parents in common want to enter the religious state.* Even when parents have gone to considerable expense in bringing up their child, in the hope of adding through him to their fortune or honor, they have no reasonable cause of complaint should he leave them to become a religious; for, says Suarez, they could not, and should not, expect their outlay and trouble to produce any nobler fruits.† We must add that, were his parents reduced to great need, a child would be obliged, even after religious profession, to assist them by every means in his power; and were their need to become extreme, he would have to quit his monastery in order to succor them, unless he could devise some other way of relieving their necessities.‡ The religious life is a school of perfection according to St. Thomas: hence, far from suppressing, it develops all the noble impulses of the human heart, and, consequently, gratitude and attachment to parents. But St. Thomas further remarks that the honor due to

---

* Suar., lib. 5, c. v, n. 3.   † Ibid., n. 14.
‡ St. Lig., *Theol. Moral.*, lib. 4, n. 67.

parents does not consist in rendering them mere bodily service, but takes in, besides, spiritual service and that respect to which their authority has a right. For this reason the religious can fulfil the commandment on honoring parents by praying for them, and paying them that tribute of respect and assistance which his calling allows. It is in this way that even persons living in the world honor their parents, some in one way, others in another, every one according to his respective condition.*

We may add that the sacrifice of their family which religious make, far from being an act of harshness, as the world sometimes unjustly calls it, is often the prompting of filial piety pushed to its farthest limits. It was thus the Princess Louisa of France tore herself away from the tenderness of her father, Louis XV, and went to shut herself up among the Carmelites, for the purpose of expiating by her penance the scandals given by her father. Who is it that knows the aching and breaking hearts of generous souls that are said to have no feeling, when, to hearken to the pleadings of grace, they find themselves compelled to leave a father and a mother, who, next to God, are the object of their warmest affections? Who can tell how much such a separation costs them? Jesus Christ alone, who has promised a hundred-fold and life everlasting to sacrifices of this nature.

---

* Div. Th., 2, 2, q. 189, a. 6.

CHAPTER XI.

IS THE CONSENT OF THEIR SUPERIORS NECESSARY FOR THOSE WHO ENTER RELIGION.

WITH regard to this question, let us begin by stating here what St. Thomas says: "Inferiors can be relieved in two ways from their obedience to superiors. In the first place, if a magistrate gives a command, and the supreme ruler of the state an opposite one, it is beyond doubt, says St. Augustine, that the order of the magistrate is to be laid aside, and the will of the sovereign to be done. Therefore, when God and a worldly ruler give us contradictory orders, God, and not the ruler, is to be obeyed. In the next place, a subject is not bound to yield obedience to a superior who commands what he has no right to command. Man is entirely dependent on God, and is bound to obey him in all things, but subjects are not wholly dependent on superiors: they owe submission only within certain limits. Thus, for instance, they are under no obligation to obey superiors in the choice of a state of life."*

---

* Div. Th., 2, 2, q. 104, a. 5.

Here is the teaching of St. Thomas, and, according to St. Liguori, it is commonly received among theologians.* It is a doctrine as logical as it is liberal. In order to draw inferences from it, we shall enter into some details. Before doing so, however, we proclaim loudly that it is no wish of ours to lessen the respect and veneration that are due to superiors. We are conscious that they hold, in regard to us, the place of God. Yet obedience has limits set to it by the hand of heaven. We must accept the divine law such as it is. We must discard neither the rights which it secures to us, nor the duties that it lays upon us.

Can a parish priest enter religion without the leave of his bishop? St. Liguori puts this question, and his answer is: "We must hold by all means that he can." In support of this answer the saint quotes canon law, St. Thomas, and the great Benedict XIV, who delivers this as certain. The illustrious pontiff, however, says that, before leaving, the pastor should, not so much indeed from duty or courtesy, as from natural law, make known his purpose to his bishop, in order that his flock may not be left without a shepherd. After that, even though the bishop should disapprove the priest's intention, the latter may still withal become a religious.† But how does the case stand with respect to clerics and other beneficiaries, who have no care of souls?

---

* *Theol. Moral.*, lib. 4, n. 68. † Ibid., n. 74.

"Here is my answer," continues St. Liguori. "Though bound by their state and by courtesy to inform the bishop of their purpose to enter religion, they commit no sin if, from reverential fear, or from an apprehension of being thwarted in their desires, they neglect to warn their ordinary, as Benedict XIV declares. It is certain that bishops cannot prevent their seminarians from entering religion. An archdeacon having entered the Society of Jesus, his Eminence, Cardinal Quirinus, complained that he had done so without his leave, and had a book printed to induce the Sovereign Pontiff of the time to declare that a cleric cannot enter religion against the will of his bishop. But the Holy Father answered, as St. Gregory had previously done in a like case, that, far from preventing ecclesiastics from such an undertaking, they are to be strengthened and urged to carry it out. Yet Benedict XIV says that if a cleric, by entering religion, were to cause great harm to the church to which he is attached, his bishop would have power to recall him."* If it is certain, as St. Liguori clearly proves, that bishops have no right to hinder clerics from embracing a religious life, what right can a family or a parish have to hinder, under futile pretexts, a person, whom grace solicits, from giving himself or herself to God?

---

* *Theol. Mor.*, lib. 4, n. 75.

The holy doctor puts also this question: "Do children sin who enter religion in spite of their parents?" To some minds his answer may sound somewhat harsh; however, its practical bearing is so great, that we would blame ourselves if we witheld it from the reader. We are so accustomed, nowadays, to listen to absurd bursts upon the interests of time and the rights of man, that we can afford to pardon a saint and doctor of the Church for speaking to us forcibly on the interests of the soul and the rights of God. Besides, we are aware that the Church found nothing to censure in the teaching of St. Liguori. Therefore, we shall neither add to nor take from this teaching; and we doubt not that Christian souls will gather it up with all the respect due to the threefold authority of holiness, learning, and experience.

"The father of Protestantism, Luther, pretended that children sinned by entering religion against the consent of their parents; but this doctrine was condemned by the Council of Toledo. That council says that girls of full twelve years, and boys of fourteen, have a perfect right to embrace the religious state without the leave of their parents. The same is taught by Saints Ambrose, Jerome, Bernard, Thomas, and Chrysostom. Theologians, also, commonly teach that a child is not bound to give up his purpose of entering religion to prevent scandal on the part of his parents; that is, to prevent them from blaspheming, from giving way to anger, or speaking against the faith.*

St. Alphonsus did not speak this way only when he delivered his views as a theologian. He also wrote as follows to a young man: "Under pretext of calming your father and mother, evil counsellors will say to you that it is a matter of conscience for you to expose your parents to lose their souls. Make no account of such scruples: if your parents wish to lose their souls, it is their concern. Tell them that you cannot, for the sake of soothing them, put your own soul in danger, by giving up your evident vocation."†

Grave authors tell us that, when parents refuse consent, their child should wait a while until his parents come to learn their duty. They say, furthermore, that, if he is sure to obtain their consent easily, it is but proper that he should not leave his home without receiving the blessing of his father and mother. This latter circumstance, however, holds only where the child has no reason to apprehend that his parents will throw unreasonable obstacles in the way of his vocation. Generally speaking, therefore, children are to be excused in practice, who leave their families for such a purpose as this without the consent of their parents.

---

* St. Lig., *Theol. Mor.*, lib. 4, n. 68.
† "Spiritual Letters," let. 13th.

But, should children at least consult their parents on the choice of a state of life, with a view to receive good advice from them?

When it is question of entering the marriage state, many theologians are of opinion that children are bound to take their parents' advice, for the reason that, in such a matter, parents have more experience than children.*

"However this may be, Father Pinamonti justly observes that, when there is question of choosing the religious state, it is neither necessary nor proper that children should take on that subject the advice of their parents; not only because the latter have no experience in the case, but, furthermore, because, led astray by their own personal interests, they become enemies, according to the expression of St. Thomas. And, in truth, it too frequently happens that parents prefer to see their children go to ruin with themselves to seeing them save their souls without them, as St. Bernard says in speaking on this subject: "O hard-hearted father!" exclaims the saint, "barbarous mother! cruel parents! unfeeling souls! you are not parents, you are murderers; for you grieve to see your son saved, and you rejoice at the sight of his eternal perdition." †

The holy doctor cites other testimonies in support of his thesis, and then continues thus:

---

* *Catech. Concil. Trid. de matrim.*, n. 3.
† *Theol. Moral.*, lib. 4, n. 68; Bernard. epist. III. Ed. Migne.

"Hence St. Thomas recommends those who are called to the religious state to avoid taking counsel of their parents about their vocation. From all this reasoning we must conclude, not only that children do not sin who follow the religious life without taking the advice of their parents, but that, ordinarily, it would be a grave mistake to inform them of their project, by reason of the danger to which they would expose themselves of being debarred from putting it into execution. And this line of action receives confirmation from the example of so many saints, who gave up the world without the knowledge, and in spite, of their parents. God approved and favored their glorious flight, even by miracles. This is also the opinion of the learned Ebbel, who says: 'When a child finds himself called by God to the religious state, and perceives that his parents are ill-disposed toward him, and, on account of their excessive carnal love for him, would throw obstacles in his way, he is under no obligation to consult them, for it will be wiser and more prudent for him to keep his intention to himself.'"* All that we have just said is taken, word for word, from St. Liguori's large work on moral theology. He adds what follows, in his short treatise on "The choice of a state of life," or on vocation: "The saints, directly they were called to leave the world, left it altogether,

---

* *Theol. Mor.*, lib. 4, n. 68.

without informing their parents. This was the conduct of St. Thomas of Aquin, St. Francis Xavier, St. Philip Neri, and St. Louis Bertrand. St. Stanislaus also made his escape without his father's permission. His brother instantly followed in pursuit, driving his carriage at full speed. As he was on the point of overtaking the holy fugitive, his horses stopped: no amount of beating could make them move on. At last Paul Kostka turned them about, and then they set off in a gallop to the town from which they had started.

"We have, besides, the example of the blessed Oringa of Valdarno, in Tuscany. Though betrothed to a young man, she secretly left her home to consecrate herself to God. Arriving at the banks of the Arno, which barred her way, she said a short prayer, and immediately saw the river part its waters, which rose on both sides like walls of crystal, and opened a dry passage to her.

"Even when parents are gifted with piety, self-interest and passion so far lead them astray, that, under one pretext or another, they make no scruple to thwart by every means the vocation of their children.

"We read, in the Life of Father Paul Segneri the Younger, that his mother, although a woman far advanced in prayer, left no stone unturned to hinder the vocation of her son, who was called to the religious life. How many other parents, that were very devout people, underwent an extraordinary change in cases of this nature, and seemed possessed by an evil spirit! So true is it that, in no circumstance, does the devil employ more formidable arms than when there is question of barring the path of persons called to the religious life.

"This doctrine will not be deemed severe by those who know that the religious vocation is one of the highest favors that God can bestow on a child or on his family. To refuse parents, therefore, the right of intercepting it, is to bind them to receive what will be their happiness and the happiness of their children. Persons intending to follow the religious life can certainly abide by the decisions that have just been quoted from St. Liguori; for the doctrine of this holy and illustrious bishop may be followed with a safe conscience, as it is easy to infer from numerous declarations of the Holy See. However, the civil law often obliges religious orders not to receive, without the previous consent of their parents, candidates that have not attained their twenty-first year, and who, if admitted before that age, might, at the request of their parents, be forced to leave the order into which they had entered. But as soon as they have reached their twenty-first year, young people may be received into religious communities or congregations against the will of their parents. The gentle St. Francis of Sales, whom even worldlings love and admire, wrote, as follows, to a young person whose parents kept her in the world against her will: " If, in regard to your vocation, you trust in those whom God has appointed your guides in domestic and temporal matters, you deceive yourself, since they have no authority to deal with such a question. Were the voice of parents of flesh and blood to be listened to in such matters, there would be few to embrace the perfection of the Christian life."*

In these days, when every one is crying out for liberty of conscience, that often is used only in behalf of evil, let us grant it to those who wish to make the holiest and best possible use of it.

---

* Gautrelet, *Traité de l'état religieux*, t. 1, p. 55.

CHAPTER XII.

IS LONG PREVIOUS PRACTICE OF VIRTUE REQUISITE FOR ENTRANCE INTO RELIGION.

THE enemies of the religious life make war on it in a multitude of ways. At times they speak of it with haughty contempt, and in language replete with insult. This, however, is not the most dangerous form of attack upon it. Such outrages hurled against a state that all the doctors of the Church, all the saints, all serious minds, have esteemed, loved, and admired, recoil upon their authors. To bring into clear light the dispositions of heretics in his time, the learned Cardinal Bellarmine had only to contrast their blasphemies against that state with the praises which the fathers of the Church had showered on that divine institution. And he observed, with good reason, that, as every pious writer has eulogized the religious life, there probably never was a heretic who did not feel irritated at the bare mention of its name.*

---

* Bellarm., *Controv. de memb. eccles. præf. de monachis.*

But, among the weapons turned against the religious life, there are some more perfidious than open hatred and insult; there are certain prejudices bearing a semblance of truth that are spread abroad in order to lead simple minds astray, and to debar them from the religious life. St. Thomas wrote a treatise on " The pestilent doctrine of those who dissuade men from entering religion." In the preface to this work, the holy doctor relates that, in his own time, new Vigilantii (Vigilantius was a heretic of the first ages of the Church) had arisen in France, who in divers ways wickedly discouraged people from entering the religious state. " These enemies," says he, " of the religious state assert, first, that no one can take upon himself, by entering religion, the practice of the counsels, unless he has previously given himself to the observance of the commandments. By such an assertion they close the path of perfection against sinners, against children, and recent converts to the faith. They say, besides, that no one can enter religion before he has consulted many persons. Now, every one can perceive what obstacles such a doctrine raises against perfection. For, men who give ear only to flesh and blood, and who always form the majority, instead of exhorting others to, will debar them from, spiritual things. The criminal attempts of these enemies of the religious state were foreshadowed by Pharaoh, who reproached

Moses and Aaron for seeking to take the people of God out of Egypt."*

The Angelical Doctor refutes these prejudices, in the work just named, and also in his Sum of Theology. In this last work he puts himself this question: "Can those who have not trained themselves in the observance of the commandments enter the religious state?" Here is the answer: "The Lord called Matthew the publican to the observance of the counsels, though he had had no practice in the commandments. It is not therefore necessary, in order to rise to the perfection of the counsels, to be practised in the commandments.† St. Paul, who among the apostles was the last to be converted to Jesus Christ, embraced evangelical perfection immediately after his marvellous conversion. Many new converts to the faith of the Church enter the religious state soon after their reception into the fold of Christ. Who would be so bad an adviser as to recommend them to remain in the world rather than seek in a monastery a shelter for their baptismal grace? Who but a silly man would attempt to make them alter their holy resolves? This suffices, then, to show how ridiculous it is to pretend that we should keep away from the religious life all those who have not for a long time observed the commandments of God."‡

---
* Opusc. 17, c. i. † St. Th., 2, 2 q. 189. a. 1. ‡ Ibid., c. iv.

As to repentant sinners, it is plain that, even after the most grievous sins, they may enter the path of the counsels. Furthermore, to speak properly, it is especially befitting for them to undertake the life of the counsels. For one has all the more reason to refuse himself what is allowable, because he often indulged in what was forbidden. And the more grievous the harm we have done to ourselves by sin, the more we ought to increase our gains by repentance. For this reason Pope Stephen, writing to one Astolphus, who had been guilty of heinous crimes, said to him: "Follow our counsel: enter a monastery." We might adduce, in support of this doctrine, many examples of the saints. Several of them, after a life of terrible sin, began immediately to practise the counsels, and shut themselves up in the most austere monasteries, without devoting any previous time to the commandments.*

"When people tell us that, before entering on the counsels, one should have a habit of keeping the commandments, it is as if they said that we should first keep the commandments imperfectly before trying to observe them fully—which is a foolish assertion. Who, then, is senseless enough to stop one that wishes to love God and his neighbor perfectly, and first restrict him to imperfect charity? Have we to fear lest a man should reach too soon perfect love for God?

---

* Opusc. 17, c. v.

"Again, who will bid him that seeks to observe continence or virginity, begin by living chastely in the married state? Who would dare to advise a person desirous of embracing poverty for the sake of Jesus Christ, first to live amid riches and observe the laws of justice, as if the possession of wealth were a preparation for the practice of poverty, whereas, on the contrary, wealth throws many obstacles in its way? Are we bound to say to a young man: Live among persons of the opposite sex or among libertines, so as to form yourself to chastity, which you will afterward observe in religion—as if it were easier to cultivate that virtue in the world than in the cloister? Those who parade such a doctrine resemble generals that, at the very outset, would expose to the severest shocks of war raw recruits that have only recently been drafted into the army.

"Yet we are willing to grant that those who, in the world, have faithfully kept the commandments will afterward be able to make greater spiritual progress in religion; but if, on the one side, the observance of the commandments in a secular life makes a man fitter for the practice of the counsels, on the other, the habit of secular life is an obstacle to the practice of perfection.* The religious state is a school that draws us away from evil, and conducts us more easily to

---

* Opusc. 17, c. vi.

perfection. Persons of feeble virtue, and but little versed in the fulfilment of God's law, have greater need than others of the means of preservation which the religious life affords: it is easier for them to shun sin in religion than it would be were they living under the freedom of the world.* Religious observance, at the same time that it removes the hindrances to perfect charity, also does away with the occasions of sin; for it is evident that fasting, watching, obedience, and other exercises of the same nature, keep a man from the excesses of intemperance, from failing in chastity, and from every other kind of sin. Entering religion, therefore, is an advantage, not only to those who have long fulfilled the commandments, since it leads them to far greater perfection, but for those also who have not done so, because, thereby, it is easier for them to keep from sin and acquire perfection.† Holy orders demand previous holiness; but the religious state is a means to holiness. The superstructure of holy orders can be laid only on foundations dried and solidified by virtue; the burden of religion of itself dries its own foundations, and relieves man from the moisture and vitiating influences of passion."‡

These last words of the Angelic Doctor are worthy of remark; and they show that we must never confound the conditions requisite for

---

* Opusc. 17, c. vii. † St. Th., 2, 2, q. 189, a. 1. ‡ Ibid., ad 3.

entering religion with those that are indispensable for taking holy orders. Deception on this point would expose us to exclude from the religious state persons who are exceedingly in need of it, and for whom that life may be strictly obligatory, as we have already stated in the fifth chapter of this section. For there are souls guilty only because they are cast among occasions, or because they have not in the world sufficient means of preservation. Give them the shelter and resources of the religious life, and they will pass their days without difficulty in the grace of God.

In concluding, we must take notice that St. Thomas speaks of penitent sinners; and it is important to remember that a constitution of Sixtus V closes the doors of religious properly so called against those who have publicly committed certain crimes, such as homicide, robbery, and others as grave, or graver still.*

However, the result of the teaching of St. Thomas is, that even souls laden with grievous and secret sins may confidently aspire to the blessings of the religious life, when, under the touch of grace, they detest their wanderings, and are sincerely resolved to expiate them far from the world in the tears of repentance.

---

* Suar., lib. 5, c. vii, n. 15.

CHAPTER XIII.

CAN CHILDREN BE ADMITTED INTO RELIGION?

This is the second question that St. Thomas puts. He answers it, at great length, both in his Sum and in his Seventeenth Short Treatise. He first says that in his time the custom of the Church was for parents to offer their children to God, and have them brought up in religious houses in the practice of the counsels. "This custom," he adds, "is sanctioned by many passages in the canons of the Church and by the examples of saints. St. Gregory, for instance, relates, in his Dialogues, that Christian parents belonging to the most distinguished families of Rome flocked to St. Benedict to place their children in his hands, in order that he might train them up for God. It was thus that Maurus and Placidus, two very promising children, were intrusted to the saint by Euticius and Tertullus, their respective fathers. From his tenderest years, St. Benedict himself, disregarding the study of human learning, and seeking only to please God, left his father's house, and every thing in the world, to devote himself to the practice of a holy life.

"It is said that the origin of this pious custom reaches as far back as the days of the apostles; and if we wish to go still higher, it rests on the authority of our blessed Lord himself. Indeed, we read in St. Matthew that children were presented to Jesus Christ, that he might lay his sacred hands upon them and pray for them. The apostles reprimanded the people who did so, and sought to send their children away, but Jesus said to them: 'Let little ones come to me, for of such is the kingdom of heaven.' (Mark x, 14.) On these words of the Gospel St. John Chrysostom says: 'If children are driven from Christ, who will deserve to go near him? Now, it is evident that we get near Jesus Christ mainly by the practice of the counsels. Children, therefore, should not be kept from Christ by hindering them from practising these counsels.'"* The Angelical next cites a passage from Origen in proof of his position; then, having spoken of St. John Baptist, who spent his youth in the desert, he ends by these words: "Not only is it allowed, but it is even very useful, that, in order to merit fully more copious graces, some should, from their earliest years, give up the world and dwell in the retirement of a monastery. Hence we read in Jeremias: 'It is good for a man when he hath borne the yoke from his youth' (Lam. iii, 27); and in the book of Proverbs, xxii, 6: 'A

---

*Opusc. 17, c. iii.

young man according to his way, even when he is old, he will not depart from it.' Hence St. Anselm puts on a level with angels those who from their youth have grown up in monasteries, while he sees only men in others who begin to lead a good life in age or the decline of their years.

"This teaching is clearly the outcome of what occurs every day among men. For, do we not see children put early to those avocations, arts, or trades, which they are to follow in after-life? Candidates for the sanctuary begin in youth to gather the knowledge which will help them later; those destined for a military career are trained to arms from their early years, and the future tradesman is apprenticed when only a boy. Why, then, should a rule, so well observed in other spheres, be neglected in the case of the religious state? Why should it not be good to accustom even children to the practices of the religious life? I say even more: when a state of life is attended with many difficulties, the greater is the need to habituate one's self from youth to overcome them."* The illustrious Suarez speaks perhaps still more to the point than St. Thomas. He demonstrates that it is allowable for a child having the use of reason to enter religion, if he wishes to do so, and if his parents raise no objection; because such a step is forbidden neither

---
* Opusc. 17, c. iii.

by natural, nor by divine, nor by ecclesiastical law.* He furthermore teaches that parents may offer their children to a religious community, to be educated and spend their lives in it; and many texts of canon law are evident proof of the statement. † Still, when a child thus offered has attained its twelfth year, if a girl, and its fourteenth, if a boy, it can recall or annul the offering, and leave the monastery; for, at that age, parents have no right to force a child against its will to enter religion, though they may very well, with its consent, offer it to God and to religion.‡

The question of right being settled, Suarez inquires into the opportuneness or propriety of such action. A Catholic, he says, can have no doubt but that, for children who have reached the age determined by the Church, it is good to enter religion, if such is their wish and inclination. It is because the Church deems such a time of life fitted for religion, that she has legislated for it. According to the ruling of the Council of Trent, religious profession cannot be made before the age of sixteen full years; but, as a year of novitiate must precede profession, it is plain that children can be admitted as novices at fifteen.§ "Theology," says Bishop Lucquet, following Lessius, "considers as an imprudent judgment ‖

---

* Suar., lib. 5, c. ii, nn. 2–7. † Ibid., c. i, n. 12.
‡ Ibid., c. ii, n. 1, et c. i, n. 13. § Ibid., lib. 5, c. iii.
‖ Lessius, *De statu vitæ eligendo*, q. 1, nn. 8 et 10.

the pretensions of those who find fault with the age fixed by the canons of the Church for taking solemn vows. It is an imprudent judgment, since it prefers its own views to the decision of popes, councils, and doctors of the Church. It is unjust; for, to retain people many years in the world against the call of God, is to expose them to trials which generally prove spiritually hurtful. To set down of one's own accord twenty, for instance, as the age for entering religion, is far from being a wise decision, for it has against it Holy Scripture, the fathers of the Church, and even reason itself." *

" A young man can now begin his noviceship at the end of his fourteenth year, and a young girl at the end of her twelfth." †

But what are we to think of admitting children into a religious house before that age? St. Thomas teaches that such admission is highly beneficial. We have already given his views on the subject. Suarez says that it is very useful for children to be received into a regular community where religious discipline and the watchfulness of superiors are in full vigor. Besides the testimony and proofs of St. Thomas, this eminent theologian alleges, in favor of his teaching, the authority of SS. Athanasius, Ambrose, Jerome and Augustine, whose words are quoted by Bellarmine. ‡

---

* Lucquet, *De la vocation*, t. ii, p. 335; Lessius, q. 2, nn. 12 et 22.
† Lessius, ibid., q. 1, n. 11.   ‡ Suar., lib. 5, c. iii, n. 7.

St. Francis of Sales, writing to Madame de Chantal, says: "As to our little ones, the younger daughters of the Lady —— I am in favor of your having them brought up in convents, with a view to leaving them there: but on two conditions. First, that the convents be good, and keep faithfully to their rule. Secondly, that, when the time for their profession comes, the children shall be carefully examined, in order to find out whether they enter on that life with piety and good-will. In placing them there, give them sweet and gentle inspirations; afterward, if they remain in the convent with such dispositions, they will be very happy, and their mother also will be very happy for having planted them in that garden of the heavenly Spouse, who will water them with a hundred thousand graces from on high." *

Euphrasia, a kinswoman of the Emperor Theodosius, being left a widow after one year of married life, had only a daughter to bear her name. To shun an alliance proposed by the emperor, she retired with her only child into Egypt, and, in her company, visited the many monasteries of men and women which then flourished in that country. One of them contained a hundred nuns, who led a life of austere penance. Euphrasia took delight in paying them frequent visits, and always had her daughter with her, who was then at that time about seven years old. Now and then the

---

* Letter 107.

superior of the convent loved to converse with the young Euphrasia, in whom she perceived precocious dispositions for piety. She attempted, in a playful manner, to discover the real sentiments of the child's young heart, and asked her one day whether she liked the convent. The child answered, with great frankness, that she was very fond of it. " Well, then," replied the superior, " if you like us, remain with us." "Indeed," answered the little girl, " I would like very much to do so, but I fear it would give pain to my mother." These words were accompanied with a holy joy, and the child's mother gave evidence of her gladness by her tears.

But matters wore a more serious aspect when the time came for leaving the monastery. The young girl then told her mother that she wished to remain, and she persisted in her resolution. As her resistance was taken for a child's freak, it was thought that, by allowing her to spend the night in the monastery, she would, on the next day, be in no humor to remain any longer. However, the next day her will was unchanged. The abbess, perceiving something supernatural in such constancy, said to the child's mother: " Madame, leave your daughter with us, grace is working in her soul." Euphrasia, whose virtue surpassed her mother's love, hereupon took her daughter before a picture of our Lord, and, with tears streaming from her eyes, said : " My Lord Jesus Christ, accept this child, since she desires only thee." Then turning to her child, she gave her much good advice and put her in the hands of the abbess. A few years later this generous mother died, after a holy life, in the same monastery, in the arms of her daughter. The young Euphrasia walked on with giant steps in the way of virtue and miracles that have given her great renown among the Greeks, and made the Church honor her as a saint.*

Perhaps some will fancy that such doctrine and such examples are out of harmony with the manners and ideas of our day. They are not. If there are communities that do not take upon themselves the care of children on account of the dangers mentioned by Suarez, or that, for solid motives, put off beyond sixteen the religious profession, in many religious societies it is nevertheless the custom, even at the present day, to receive children, to train them from youth to Christian perfection, and thus save them from the corrupting influences of the world. Sometimes this is the best, and almost the only, means that certain religious communities have to recruit the subjects of which they are in need.

There are also, in our day, Christian parents capable of sacrificing to God all that they hold most dear. The number of such parents will increase when the advantages and excellence of

---

* "Lives of the Fathers," lib. 2, c. vii.

the religious life will be better understood, and when people will relish still more the words of our Lord: "Seek ye first the kingdom of heaven and its justice." (Matt. vi, 33.)

Men who have experience of souls know well what a religious community can do for a child whom vice has not yet robbed of its innocence, or of its yearning for virtue. Read the reports of the apostolic schools where, in knowledge and in virtue, grow up future missioners, who, with their childish hearts, already take in the whole world. Could they who find the teaching of St. Thomas strange inhale the perfume of piety, candor, and grace, which some religious boarding-schools breathe out at the close of a scholastic year; if they could get a close view of the supernatural loveliness which the solitude of a monastery sheds in a few months over these young souls, they would, with the holy doctor, acknowledge that "it is good for a man to bear the yoke of the Lord from his tenderest years." Alas! these flowers that have opened and bloomed, under the breath of God, in the shade of the cloister, are no sooner exposed to the parching blasts of the world, than they fade and lose all their glory. Sometimes only a few days spent in the world are enough to blast these fairest of hopes. As soft wax, the child, says the poet, receives every impress of vice: *Cereus in vitium flecti;** hence

---

* Horace, "Art of Poetry," line 163.

nothing better can be done for him than to separate him from every scandal and every occasion of sin, by multiplying around him supports for his weakness. This is what the religious state does.

Give a child forever what a religious boarding-school supplies for a few years, and you will see it grow up in happiness and sanctity. Wherefore, when parents notice in their child an early taste for religious perfection, far from crushing such consoling dispositions by endless delays, they should foster them with the fondest care. Is it reasonable, under pretence of testing a vocation, to oblige a child to spend a long time amid the dangers of the world, to witness all its vanities, and share in the treacherous joys of its festivities? Could even the most solid virtue resist assaults of this kind? We acknowledge, indeed, that prudence is supremely necessary; but, had the holy doctors, whose teaching we are here laying down, less of that virtue than we have? Why should we endeavor to be wiser than the Church, who allows the religious profession at sixteen years of age, and entrance into religion at any age?

When there is question of marrying a young woman, great eagerness is shown; and still even then an irrevocable engagement is contracted, and one, too, that involves the most serious consequences. But when leave is asked to enter religion, there is always time enough to do it later, and it is ever too soon to give one's self to

God. Yet, it is only after long and serious trial that a person embracing the religious state is called upon to assume the obligation of remaining in it forever. We should not be wiser than it behooveth, says St. Paul. (Rom. xii, 3.) Christian souls should abhor the prudence of the flesh, which, according to the same apostle, is the death of the soul. (Rom. viii, 6.) For this reason St. John Chrysostom complains bitterly of parents who are unwilling that their children should enter young into religion. He attacks and refutes all the pretexts by which they seek to justify their conduct. We take a pleasure in laying his splendid pages before the reader:—

"What assurance have you that your children will reach mature age? Many are hurried out of life by a sudden death. But, even supposing that you have such certainty, who will be responsible for their early years?* No one guarantees that they will continue virtuous. On the other hand, parents reply: Who can certify to us that our son will persevere in religion? And who tells you," answers the eloquent doctor, "that he will not persevere? Why have you not the same fears with respect to the literary career, or any other career of the kind, about which your fears would be far more in place? For, in the monastic state, among many aspirants, few fall away; whereas, among the seekers after eloquence,

---

* *Adv. oppugnat. vit. monast.*, lib. 3, c. xi.

only a small number meet with success. In the career of letters the inability of the child, the engagements of his father, the absence of the necessary resources to cover expense, the hatred and jealousy of fellow-students, and a thousand other obstacles, prevent a candidate from reaching the goal. And when that goal has been reached, difficulties, in still greater number, arise. The enmity of a chief in office, the envy of a colleague, unfavorable circumstances, want of friends, and poverty, shipwreck a young man's prospects in the very port itself. The case is not the same in the monastic life. There only one thing is required: noble, generous courage. He who has that cannot fail to reach the goal of virtue. Having under your eyes and, so to speak, in your hands, hopes so grand, can you be afraid, can you be discouraged, while, when there is question of a route crossed by so many obstacles, you drive away all fear, your courage redoubles the more the difficulties thicken around you? Can there be anything more senseless than such behavior? As regards the religious life, no sooner has your son crossed its threshold, than directly your head is filled with the strangest thoughts springing from your discouragement alone. But not long ago you used to say: 'Can one not remain in the world, and still be saved?' Is it really the same man who at one time has full confidence in the possibility of salvation, even amid all the cares and turmoil of the world, and afterward trembles for the solitary that has been freed from his barriers? You maintained that a man may save his soul in a city: with much more reason will he be able to do so by retiring into solitude."*

" But my son is young and weak. It is just for that reason," continues St. Chrysostom, " that he should be less exposed, and more surrounded with means of protection. You upset things altogether; for you throw into the battle of life in the world those whose years, whose weakness and inexperience, have most to fear from the combat. You act like an officer who would order a raw soldier, that cannot yet stand the brunt of war, to throw himself for that very reason into the thickest of the fight, and to command the action. He who waits for the close of life to embrace virtue, spends the remnant of his days in washing out with his tears the sins of his youth; but he who went early into the arena does not stop to dress his wounds: in his very trial-contest he wins signal victories and glorious rewards. It is now your place to determine what rank you wish your son to occupy in heaven."†

This long and remarkable passage is taken, word for word, from St. Chrysostom.

---

* *Adv. oppugnat. vit. monast.*, lib. 3, c. xiii. † Ibid., c. xvii.

CHAPTER XIV.

IS IT PROPER TO DELIBERATE A LONG TIME, AND TO CONSULT MANY PERSONS BEFORE ENTERING RELIGION.

"When there is question of entering religion in order to lead a life at once more perfect and more secure against the dangers of this world, it is astonishing," says St. Liguori, "to what a degree people of the world carry their pretensions. They insist that, before coming to such a determination, long deliberation is essential; there must be no haste in the execution of the project, so as to gain a certainty that the call comes really from God, and not from the evil spirit. They do not speak in this way when some high office in the state is to be accepted, which is attended with so many dangers for the soul. Then they do not require the aspirant to go through so many ordeals in order to test the divine origin of his call. This is not the way in which the saints speak. St. Thomas asserts that, even though a religious vocation did come from the devil, it ought to be followed as an excellent counsel from an enemy."*

---

* "The Choice of a State of Life," 2, 2.

Here is the passage of the Angelical to which St. Liguori refers: "When Satan, hiding his malice, says or does anything that suits the good angels, any error which may follow from it is not very dangerous. Later on, when he will attempt to make use of his deceit for an evil purpose, we must be extremely on our guard, so as not to listen to his suggestions. Were the devil, then, to urge any one to enter religion there would be no danger in following the impulse, as it is a good suggestion in itself, and such as the holy angels might make. Afterward, however, we should have to be on the watch to protect ourselves against pride and the many other dangerous insinuations of the enemy of our salvation. God often uses the malice of the spirits of darkness for the good of his saints, whose struggles and victories he crowns; and it is thus that holy souls make a sport of the devil. Still we must keep in mind that, were the devil to infuse into one a desire to enter religion, such desire would beget no result, unless God drew the soul to himself by his own divine grace."*

"Things that are certain need no discussion," says the same holy doctor. "Those whose duty it is to receive into religion a subject who presents himself for admission, may not be aware of his intention in seeking admission: whether he comes for his own spiritual benefit, or whether

---
* Div. Th., opusc. 17, c. x.

he comes, as it sometimes happens, to spy and do some harm, or, again, whether he is suited for the religious state. In order that those empowered to admit may solve these questions judiciously, they must subject the candidate to trial: and this trial is prescribed by the Church and by the constitutions of every religious order. But persons having the intention to enter a religious order are in no doubt with regard to that intention. They have therefore no need of deliberation, especially when they have no reason to mistrust their bodily strength; and this they will have abundance of time to test during the year of noviceship." *

It is said that, when an undertaking is liable to failure, we should proceed in it with great caution and reflection. This is true where the undertaking is in itself dangerous, and often exposed to serious risks. In that case mature deliberation is imperative in order to eschew all danger, or even to forego the project altogether; but, when risks are rare, there is no need of much hesitation. Ordinary watchfulness will suffice to ward off every mishap. " He that observes the wind, shall not sow: and he that considers the clouds, shall never reap." (Eccl. xi, 4.) "The slothful man says: There is a lion in the way, and a lioness in the roads." (Prov. xxvi, 13.) But there are enterprises, sound and solid in themselves, which still withal turn out badly, because those who

---

* Div. Th., opusc. 17, c. x.

embark in them are wanting in perseverance. No one should allow himself to be thwarted, or to defer his entrance into religion, on the plea that lengthy deliberation is necessary, for the reason that many have given up the religious life, and afterward became worse than they had previously been; otherwise we should never embrace the Catholic faith, for it is written: "It had been better for them not to have known the way of justice than, after they have known it, to turn back from that holy commandment which was delivered to them." (2 Pet. ii, 21.)

People say also that, if a work is from God, it will not come to naught. (Acts v, 38.) Heretics, misunderstanding this passage of Scripture, endeavor to base two errors on it. The first is, that bodies which are subject to corruption do not come from God; and the second is, that he who has the grace of God cannot lose it. According to these heretics, then, since Judas by his treachery excluded himself from the number of apostles, we must conclude that his vocation was not divine. Well, the strange reasoning indulged in by the enemies of the religious state is equally absurd. Here it is: If he who enters religion afterward abandons it, there is proof that God did not call him to it, and that the zeal of those who advised him to take the step did not proceed from God.* St. Thomas upsets this

---

* St. Th., opusc. c. x.

senseless argument, and closes by saying that there are some who have received a religious vocation from God, though afterward they do not persevere in it.

It is no shame to attempt to embrace the state of perfection and to fail in the enterprise. The world, that employs every means to stifle the projects of souls aspiring to a holy life, seeks, nevertheless, to make a reproach out of an unsuccessful undertaking of this nature. At all costs, it wishes to prevent men from even making the attempt. No matter, however, what may be the ideas of that world, even the few months spent in a religious house by those who do not persevere, are often fruitful in consolations, in pious exercises, in acts of virtue, and they are sheltered from the dangers and the sins in which life in the world usually abounds.

To those who are of opinion that, if a vocation came from God, delays and obstacles would not be able to destroy it, St. Liguori replies in his turn: "The lights that God sends us are fleeting, not permanent. This is what led St. Thomas to say that divine calls to a more perfect life must be followed without delay: *quanto citius.*" *

"St. John Chrysostom, quoted by the Angelical, says that, when God favors us with similar inspirations, he does not wish us to hesitate a moment to follow them. Why so? Because the Lord loves to

---

* "The Choice of a State," 2, 2.

see us docile; and the more prompt we are, the more he opens his hand to fill us with blessings. But delays give him great displeasure. God then closes his hand and withholds his graces, so that he who puts off corresponding to his vocation finds it difficult to follow it, and easily gives it up altogether. "Hence," adds St. Chrysostom, "when the devil cannot rob one of his resolution to consecrate himself to God, he endeavors to persuade him, at least, to defer its execution, and he considers it a great gain to obtain a delay of a day, or even of an hour; for, if, during that day or hour, a new occasion should present itself for delay, it will be less difficult for him to obtain more and more procrastination. In this way does the devil act until the person called by God, finding himself weaker and less influenced by grace, ends by yielding altogether and renouncing his vocation. By such delays how often has not the enemy destroyed a vocation! For this reason St. Jerome, addressing those who are called to abandon the world, urges them to esape as soon as possible."* "Hurry," says he; "cut, rather than untie, the rope which binds your boat to the shore;"† that is to say, break as quickly as possible the bonds which fasten you to the world.

"Peter and Andrew," says St. Thomas, "directly they were called by our Lord, left their nets on the spot to follow him; and St. Chrysostom says,

---

* "The Choice of a State," 2, 2.   † Hieron., epist. 53 ad Paulin.

to their praise, that, hearing the orders of Christ in the midst of their occupations, they made no delay in executing them. They did not say, 'Let us go back to our homes and see our friends,' but, leaving everything, they followed him."*

These words were not spoken by the saints with a view to make people enter the religious life rashly, but as a preservative against worldly prejudices, and against the delays in which nature readily delights, but which often extinguish the grace of heaven.

St. Liguori himself observes that the prudence of a confessor may sometimes delay entrance into religion,† and Suarez wishes him who enters religion to do so with full knowledge of the step that he is taking. It is not enough to know that the religious state is the best in itself; we must also compare with that state the one who wishes to follow it, and see whether he has sufficient health, or is in the proper circumstances for taking such a determination. What is best in itself is not always the best for every individual.‡ "But," adds the learned theologian, "in this deliberation we must take account, not of our strength only, but we must likewise consider the assistance of God on whom we are bound to rely. Cajetan remarks, with reason, that he who intends to become a religious must trust with firm hope in

---

* Div. Th., opusc. 17, c. ix, et 2, 2, q. 189, a. 10.
† *Praxis confess.*, n. 92. ‡ Suar., lib. 5, c. viii, n. 2.

divine grace. Every one may rely on it; for, if God calls even those who do not seek him, much more will he protect and sustain those whose sole purpose is to please him."* This proves the great delusion of persons who, from a fear of not persevering, can never bring themselves to a full determination to follow the divine call. "He who gives the grace to will," Lessius tells them, "will also grant the grace to accomplish. There will not be wanting to you an abundance of grace that will help you to do easily and joyfully what God requires of you; but take care that you be not wanting to yourself."† Suarez further remarks, with many theologians, that every one should look upon the religious state as suiting him, as long as he has not acquired a certainty of the contrary, either by some evident reason, or by his own personal experience. For, the watchfulness of superiors, the removal of occasions of sin, holy examples, frequent hearing of the word of God, the consolations which the Lord lavishes on religious,—all this abundance of help renders easy the obligations of a state which would be above the strength of a man living in the midst of the world.‡

Should we consult many persons before entering religion? "To lay down as a principle that many should be consulted, would be to raise," says St. Thomas, "a great obstacle against the purpose of those intending to follow the path of perfection.

---

* Suar., lib. 5, c. viii, n. 2.   † Lessius, q. 7, n. 85.   ‡ Ibid., n. 2.

Every sensible person will be of this opinion; for the advice of carnal men, who always form the greater number, turns away from, rather than exhorts to, spiritual goods."* It is not then necessary to consult much. But should we consult at all? The answer of St. Thomas is, that, " in matters which are certain, there is no need of counsel: *In his quæ certa sunt, non requiritur consilium;* and it is certain that, putting out of question the aspirant, entrance into religion, considered in itself, is a higher good. To doubt of it would be to give the lie to Jesus Christ, who made a counsel of it."† There is, therefore, no need of consulting in this matter, as Suarez observes.‡

But are we to consult in order to find out whether our desire to enter religion comes from God? As we have already said, St. Thomas is of opinion there is no obligation to do so; for, even though the desire came from the devil, it were good to carry it out. Suarez also says that, in itself and ordinarily, the desire of the religious state is from the Holy Ghost. It should therefore be accepted, and there is no need to consult about it, unless some accidental circumstances render the desire suspicious; yet, when it is to be put into execution, it may be necessary to take advice, and my opinion is, continues Suarez, that, as a general rule, advice ought to be taken.§

---

* St. Th., opusc. 17, c. i.   † Id., 2, 2, q. 189, a. 10.
‡ Suar., lib. 5, c. viii, n. 2.   § Ibid., n. 4.

"If a person has some special impediment," says the Angelical, "such as a bodily infirmity, debts, or any other hindrance of the kind, and if he has to decide how he shall enter religion, and on what order he shall fix his choice, he should reflect and ask advice of those who may help him to pursue his purpose, but not of those who might attempt to divert him from it. It is said in Holy Writ (Ecclus. xxxvii, 12): 'Treat not with a man without religion concerning holiness, nor with an unjust man concerning justice.'"*

Suarez, following St. Thomas, wishes us to consult virtuous men who are free from human affection with regard to those who ask their advice, who have right views of a perfect life and of the religious state, and even, if possible, some experience of it. Let this consultation, he adds, be prudent and serious, as the importance of the matter requires it to be, but let it not be drawn out to endless lengths. Protracted counsel is not called for, and, as a general thing, it is an obstacle to a divine vocation, and the source of many dangers. †

We have now answered, in the words of the doctors of the Church, the questions bearing on the state of tendency to perfection. It remains to say a word on the state of perfection in exercise or practice.

---

* Div. Th., 2, 2, q. 189, a. 10. † Suar., lib. 5, c. viii, n. 2.

ARTICLE II.

The State of Perfection in Practice.

We have to solve here the three following questions:—

1. Is episcopacy the most perfect of the states of the Christian life?

2. Is the state of priests having charge of souls more perfect than the religious state?

3. What are the marks and conditions of a vocation to the priesthood?

St. Thomas, St. Liguori, and Suarez will furnish us answers to these questions.

CHAPTER I.

IS EPISCOPACY THE MOST PERFECT STATE OF THE CHRISTIAN LIFE.

WE have first to remark, with St. Thomas, that, "to constitute a state of perfection, there is need of a lasting obligation, contracted with a certain solemnity, to perform works of perfection. Now, these two requisites are found in the religious state and in episcopacy. And, indeed, real religious bind themselves by vow to abstain from the goods of this world, which they might have used without any sin; and they do this, in order to devote themselves with greater freedom to the service of God, in which consists the perfection of this present life. Furthermore, they take this obligation upon them with some solemnity, namely, by their profession and the blessing of the Church. Bishops also bind themselves to works of perfection, in assuming the pastoral charge, which entails for the pastor the duty of giving his life for his flock. To this obligation is added the solemnity of episcopal consecration."*

We find, therefore, in the religious state and in episcopacy, the two conditions demanded to

---

* Div. Th., 2, 2, q. 184, a. 5.

constitute a state of perfection. But each of these states is distinguished, one from the other, in that the religious state, as we have already pointed out, "is instituted mainly for the acquirement of perfection through certain exercises which do away with the impediments to perfect charity."* This is the language of St. Thomas and of Suarez. "The religious state is therefore a school in which one trains himself to seek and aim at perfection;"† while the chief object of the state of bishops is to work with zeal for the salvation of the neighbor." ‡

"The end for which episcopacy was instituted is to enlighten and perfect others, as St. Denis teaches, and as we infer from the words of our Lord: 'You are the salt of the earth: you are the light of the world. Neither do men light a candle and put it under a bushel, but upon a candlestick, that it may shine to all that are in the house.' (Matt. v, 13–15.) Consequently he who has received that order, though he should be perfect, does not receive from his state itself the means to acquire it for himself personally, but he receives from it the means to exercise perfection and to communicate it to others."§

Having now set down wherein the religious state and episcopacy agree and differ, we can more easily examine which of the two states is the more perfect.

---

* Suar., lib. 1, c. xiv, n. 4.   † Ibid.   ‡ Ibid., c. iii.   § Ibid., c. vii.

"No one," says St. Thomas, "is allowed to pass from a more perfect to a less perfect state, for that would be to look backward. But one can pass from the religious state to episcopacy. Therefore the state of bishops is more perfect than that of religious."* Here the comparison, as Suarez observes, is between states, and not persons.† The greater perfection of the state of bishops is proved from councils and the testimony of the fathers, who claim that bishops are not only in a state of perfection, but furthermore on an eminence that no other state can equal.‡

Here is what the fathers say: "There is nothing greater in the Church than a bishop; for he is consecrated to God for the salvation of the whole world."§ "Bishops are the pillars that sustain the Church; they bear its weight on their shoulders."‖ "There is nothing more sublime than bishops."¶ "No ministry is dearer to God than theirs." These last words are from St. John Chrysostom. This holy doctor, in contrasting bishops with religious, says that bishops need higher sanctity, and he develops this idea at great length.** Indeed, Suarez teaches, with St. Thomas, that "episcopacy presupposes perfection in him who is raised to it, whereas the religious state presupposes nothing of the kind. Hence in the Council of Trent it is said: "According to the decrees of

---

* Div.Th., 2, 2, q. 184, a. 7.   † Suar., lib. 1, c. xviii, n. 1.
‡ Ibid., 2.   § Ign. Mart. apud. Suar., ibid., 6.
‖ Athan., ibid.   ¶ Ambros., ibid., 77.   ** Chrysost., ibid.

the venerable fathers, let no one be chosen to govern churches, a burden formidable to the shoulders even of angels, save those who are most worthy of the office: *qui maxime digni*. But in religion imperfect people and newly converted sinners are received, in order that they may tend to, and reach, perfection."*

Hence we have to conclude, with Suarez, that in itself it is good to desire, to seek for, and to vow, the religious state, but that the same cannot be done for episcopacy: for there would be danger lest the desire for episcopacy should be accompanied by presumption, ambition, or attachment to the things of this world, so that, generally speaking, and in itself, such a desire is not praiseworthy, nor can it be counselled; and for that very reason it is not a matter to be vowed.† "It seems presumptuous," says St. Thomas, "to aim at ruling over others in order to do them good."‡

Still it would not be intrinsically bad to bind one's self by vow to episcopacy, without any view to the temporal advantages which accompany that office: and this would be far more allowable where the episcopal dignity would entail all manner of privations, as was the case in the early Church, or as it is to-day in many foreign missions. "I speak," adds Suarez, "of the

---

* Suar., lib. 1, c. xviii, n. 9.   † Ibid., n. 11.
‡ Div. Th., 2, 2, q. 185, a. 1.

vow to accept the office; for that vow leaves to superiors the care of determining the worthiness or unworthiness of him who makes that vow, and consequently it wards off from him the danger of presumption. But to seek to become a bishop, even with all the limitations that we have mentioned, is to deem one's self fit for that high duty. Now, this is dangerous: it cannot be counselled, nor be vowed. There is, however, one case in which the seeking to become a bishop would be excusable. It is when, some particular church being deprived of her bishop, it would be difficult to find a successor, on account of severity of climate, distance, or imminent danger of death in that diocese. In such circumstances it might even be an act of perfection to offer one's self for the episcopal office in such a place."*

---

* Suar., lib. 1, c. xviii, n. 12.

CHAPTER II.

IS THE STATE OF PRIESTS HAVING CHARGE OF SOULS MORE PERFECT THAN THE RELIGIOUS STATE.

In the first place, we suppose, with Suarez, that pastors are not in the state of tendency to perfection; that is, that they are not religious. For, in virtue of their functions, they are not bound to practise the counsels of poverty and of obedience; and their office, in itself, has not for scope to lead them to perfection, but by their ministry to promote the perfection of the faithful.*

We suppose, in the second place, that bishops have the pastoral charge in a far nobler and more perfect degree than parish priests. This is evident. The bishop's dignity and office are distinct from the office and power of a priest; and this distinction is of divine institution, of divine right. The bishop differs from other priests in that he occupies a higher rank and order.†

This being laid down, let us now come to our question: Are priests having charge of souls in a loftier state of perfection than religious?

---

* Suar., lib. I, c. xvii, n. 19.   † Ibid., n. 21.

St. Thomas, having quoted a passage from canon law, which permits a secular priest to enter religion in case the Holy Ghost urges him thereto, concludes with the following words: "It appears that religious are more perfect than archdeacons and than priests having care of souls." He next enters into distinctions, which to us appear calculated to elucidate the inquiry:—

"In a pastor of souls three things can be considered: his state, the sacrament of order which he has received, and the office that he fills. By state he is secular, by order a priest, and by office he has care of souls. If, alongside of this parish priest, we place a religious who is also a priest, and has care, too, of souls, as it often happens, particularly in the case of regular canons, he will be equal to that pastor in orders and office, inasmuch as he is a priest, and has charge of souls as well as the pastor; but he will surpass him in state, because the pastor is a secular, and the religious is a regular. When the religious is a priest without care of souls, he is still superior to the parish priest by his state, which excels the former's state; he is inferior to him in functions, and equal to him in priesthood. It remains, then, for this last case, to examine which is the better: superiority of state, or superiority of functions. To determine the inquiry, two things have to be considered, namely: the moral goodness and the difficulties of the religious state, and of the care of souls. The moral goodness of the religious state is greater than that of the parish priest's state, because the religious binds himself to consecrate all his life to striving after perfection, whereas the pastor does not bind himself, as does the bishop, to devote all his life to the care of souls. Wherefore, in regard to parish clergy, the religious state is as the holocaust to a mere sacrifice. A sacrifice is less perfect than a holocaust. Hence, we read in canon law this text, which is taken from the Fourth Council of Toledo: "Bishops must leave free to enter monasteries those clerics who wish to become religious, for they seek to embrace a better life."

"It is well understood that here, too, we consider only the states themselves, and not the persons who enter them. There are pastors who, on account of the charity wherewith they are filled, are more perfect than religious that are not fervent.

"But, if we now compare the difficulties to be met with in the religious state with those attendant on the care of souls, it is more arduous to lead a holy life amid the care of souls than it is in the religious state, by reason of the dangers by which the exercise of such a ministry is surrounded. On the other hand, the religious life is more painful to nature, on account of the various practices which it imposes.

"If now we take a religious who is not a priest, a lay brother, for instance, it is clear that, in point of dignity, he will be inferior to a priest. For, by the reception of holy orders a man is appointed to those most august ministries whereby Jesus Christ himself is served in the sacrament of the altar,—ministries which demand greater interior holiness than does the religious state. Wherefore, all else being equal, a cleric in holy orders, who would do anything contrary to holiness, would sin thereby more grievously than a religious who is not in orders."*

In the foregoing remarks we merely rendered, as clearly as it was in our power, the ideas of St. Thomas. Let us now hearken to Suarez:—

"The state of parish priests and the state of religious can be contrasted from two different points of view, according as we consider them in themselves, or with reference to man. Taken with reference to ourselves, the question comes to this: Which of these two states can a man choose in preference to the other, as contributing more efficaciously to acquire purity of conscience, to progress in virtue and the worship of God, and to win eternal life? From this point of view, there is no doubt that the religious state is better, more perfect, and more advantageous. So that, the more spontaneously and readily we enter religion, the more prudent and perfect is our

---

* Div. Th., 2, 2, q. 184, a. 8.

action; but, on the other hand, we are all the more secure in the care of souls, the less has been our ardor to enter upon it of our own accord. For this reason, St. Gregory did not content himself with exhorting religious to accept a cleric who asked to be admitted among them, but he wrote to them these words: 'Urge that cleric, and encourage him in every possible way with admonitions full of tenderness, so that the ardor of his desire may not grow cool.' And he added words deserving of notice here: 'Let him not implicate himself anew in the tumult of church affairs, since, in separating himself from the whirl of worldly cares, he aspires to that calm repose which is found in the harbor of a monastery.'

"From all this we draw only one conclusion, and it is, that the religious state is a state of tendency to perfection, whereas such is not the case with the care of souls. This latter state is not as safe as the religious state: no one can deny it. The comparison instituted between these two states, considering them in reference to man, is more moral and practical. It enlightens those who have to make choice of a state of life."* From another standpoint, we could also inquire whether the state of parish priests viewed in itself contributes more to the glory of God, requires by itself more perfect works, and consequently outstrips the religious state. From this point of view, we

---

* Suar., lib. I, c. xxi, n. 5.

can say that, speculatively, it is more perfect than the religious state; but this superiority is rather speculative, as I have just said, than practical. Indeed, though it is true that the care of souls demands greater perfection, and though the works that it necessitates are of high merit when properly performed, nevertheless, in practice, it is hard to comply with this latter condition—*difficillime et raro*—for the reason, that in that state obstacles to perfection are not removed as they are in religion."*

"But, besides all this, the religious state does not exclude priesthood, and it aids the growth of charity toward God and toward our neighbor. It does not, therefore, necessarily confine itself to procuring the personal perfection of him who enters it, but it serves also to enlighten and perfect others. The perfect charity which it fosters, and leads religious to acquire, enkindles zeal." †

The foregoing remarks make us feel the necessity of not applying to the religious career those rules that are to be followed when we advise or allow a person to enter the clerical state. In itself, the religious state is safer; and, as we have already shown, St. Thomas teaches that those who encourage others to enter it, not only do not sin, but merit a glorious reward. The holy doctor adds that the religious state is admirably suited to repentant sinners, that there is no need of long

---

* Suar., lib. I, c. xxi, n. 6.   † Ibid., n. 8.

deliberation before embracing it, and that vocation to the priesthood should not be compared with the religious vocation.

Let us listen to St. Liguori: "When a young man," says he, "wishes to become a secular priest, his confessor must not easily give consent, unless he has acquired a long and convincing experience of the young man's purity of intention, of his knowledge, or of his capacity to acquire it. Secular priests are under even greater obligations than religious, and still, withal, they continue exposed to the dangers of the world. Hence, in order that a priest may be good in the world, he must have led a very exemplary life before his ordination. Without that, he would lay himself open to imminent danger of damnation, especially if he took orders to obey parents who had nothing higher than worldly motives in view."* For this reason, we consider it useful to go here into some details with reference to the qualities and conditions that an aspirant to the sublime dignity of the priesthood should possess. In this matter, too, St. Liguori will once more be our guide, and, while listening to his words, the faithful will learn greater respect for the priest. For the eminence and holiness of the priesthood are better understood, when we know what perfect dispositions Catholic theologians require in those who intend to receive holy orders.

---

* St. Lig., *Praxis confess.*, n. 93.

CHAPTER III.

WHAT ARE THE SIGNS AND CONDITIONS OF A VOCATION TO HOLY ORDERS.

"THE chief signs of a vocation to the priesthood," says the holy doctor whose views we are unfolding, "are suitable knowledge, a good life, and purity of intention. First, suitable knowledge,* or the talent necessary to acquire it.† It were a grievous sin to receive ordination in such ignorance as would render one altogether unfit to perform the duties of holy orders.‡ Secondly, a holy life. It is of this condition that the holy Council of Trent speaks, when it says: 'Let bishops know that they must raise to orders only those who are worthy of them, and whose commendable life is an old age.' (Sess. 23, c. xii.) The apostle, too, forbids the ordaining of neophytes; and not only of neophytes in age, but also of neophytes in perfection, as St. Thomas explains.

"The same doctor adds likewise: 'Sacred orders demand previous probity of life.' And in another place he says: 'To exercise holy orders

---

* St. Lig., lib. 6, n. 802.   † Id., *Praxis confess.*, n. 93.
‡ Ibid., n. 791, *quæritur* 2.

properly, it is not enough to be good in a low degree—excellence is required.' And the reason of it is this: those who receive holy orders are, by their dignity, raised above the faithful; therefore they should be raised above them also by their merits and sanctity."* " Reason and the authority of theologians and doctors prove that, for him who is raised to the dignity of holy orders, the ordinary and actual state of grace is not sufficient; he furthermore requires an habitual state of grace, surpassing the usual level of that state—*præcellens et habitualis.* 'The burden of sacred orders ought not to be laid,' says St. Thomas, 'except on walls that have been dried by holiness.' St. Chrysostom had said before him that far higher virtue is requisite for priests than for religious." †

This habitual state of grace required for the reception of sacred orders should, generally speaking, be known from an experience of some length, as is clear from passages of St. Liguori, which follow those that we are quoting:—

"The third condition, or the third sign, of vocation to the priesthood is a right intention; that is to say, a desire to labor for the glory of God and the salvation of souls, and not for one's own glory or personal interests."‡

" He who, without a vocation evidenced by such signs, would intrude on the holy ministry,

---
* St. Lig., lib. 6, n. 802. † Ibid., n. 67. ‡ Ibid., n. 802.

could not be excused from a grievous sin of presumption."* "Yet, in order that he who seeks promotion to holy orders may be free from guilt, it is enough if, with a right intention, though not certain that he has a call from God, he presents himself to his bishops for examination and trial."†

"Now, the Council of Trent commands bishops to inquire carefully into the education, morals, and learning of aspirants to holy orders, before promoting them. In this **examination and trial**, bishops must, from the testimony of reliable men, acquire a certainty, not only that the candidate is not bad, but, furthermore, that he is positively good, that he gives himself to the practice of the spiritual life, that he is assiduous in visiting churches, that he frequents the sacraments, prays, shuns the world, keeps only good company, is devoted to study, and modest in his dress."‡

When a young man possesses these three principal marks of vocation to the ecclesiastical state enumerated by St. Liguori, it is evidently a good work to furnish him means to follow that vocation. The saints always did so. As they were firm in refusing orders to the unworthy, so were they zealous in favoring true vocation.

Since, as St. Liguori assures us, a young man who is not certain that he has a call from God, who has aptitudes for the ecclesiastical state, is virtuous in conduct, and impelled by proper

---

* St. Lig., lib. 6, n. 8:3.   † Ibid., n. 72.   ‡ Ibid., n. 803.

motives, can, without any sin, present himself for examination and trial to a bishop,—it is therefore not forbidden to stir up in a pious child a sincere desire for God's glory and the salvation of souls, to foster his happy dispositions, and to afterward present him to a bishop for examination and holy orders. If thereby we have reasonable hope of giving a saintly priest to the Church, we perform an excellent act. There are truly Christian mothers who, by unceasing prayer to God, and by most vigilant spiritual care of their sons, seek to obtain for and decide in these children a vocation to the priesthood. Why is the number of such mothers not more numerous? Although it is stripped of those temporal advantages which surrounded it in by-gone days, has the priesthood lost anything of that transcendent glory which Jesus Christ has bestowed upon it? Is it not, on the contrary, all the more deserving of our admiration and devotedness, because it gives a man a closer resemblance to Jesus in his poverty, and to his persecuted apostles? Many priests do, for the virtuous children of their parish, what the pious mothers of whom we have just spoken do for their sons. They choose out of their flock the portion of God, which ought to be the best. Hence, before determining their choice, they take into consideration, above all, not the talents, but the pure life of those whom they destine for the service of the altar. And, indeed, what can talents without virtue accomplish for the glory of God? "Knowledge puffs up, but charity edifies." (1 Cor. viii, i.)

We also witness in our times those admirable works, whose object is to give a clerical education to poor, but virtuous, children. Among these works some offer a twofold advantage, that cannot be too highly valued: they prepare at once for the priestly and the religious life. With the resources which these establishments furnish, a young man without worldly means may easily, for the salvation of souls, become a priest, and procure for himself every means of sanctification that the religious state can bestow. The noble institution of the apostolic schools which our Holy Father, Pope Pius IX, has enriched with indulgences, brings up, *gratis*, pious children who are destined for missionary countries. This institution has already, in France and Belgium, five houses under the care of the fathers of the Society of Jesus. Many other religious, such as Capuchins, Premonstratensians, and Augustinians, prepare children for the secular and the regular clergy. The missionaries of the Sacred Heart of Issoudun in France, the Oblates of Mary, and others, have also their apostolic schools. May God bless these grand undertakings; may he multiply, in the Church of his Son, Jesus Christ, good priests and holy religious, who form one of its brightest glories!

SECOND PART.

THE CHOICE OF A STATE OF LIFE AND VOCATION.

PRELIMINARY NOTIONS.

IS EVERY MAN FREE TO CHOOSE THE STATE OF LIFE THAT SUITS HIM.

HAVING made known, as correctly and as clearly as we were able, the nature and advantages of the divers states of the Christian life, it remains for us to treat of the choice that the faithful may or should make.

And here, at the very outset, a question of the highest importance presents itself: "Does God call every child of the Church to a special state of life? Does he lay on every one a sort of obligation to embrace some determined state?" Or, in other words: "Is a man free to choose for himself, and as he pleases, that state of the Christian life which he prefers?"

We have found this question discussed in the learned Cornelius à Lapide, and we shall borrow from him this entire chapter. Henceforward, however, we shall say nothing of the priesthood or of episcopacy. In the foregoing pages we have laid down all that is most necessary to be known in reference to vocation to the ecclesiastical state: it were, consequently, superfluous to return to the subject in this Second Part. With these statements let us enter into the inquiry.

"'I would that all men were even as myself,' says St. Paul (1 Cor. vii, 7), that is to say, living in celibacy, 'but every one has his proper gift from God' (ibid.), namely: conjugal chastity, or virginity, or the chastity of widowhood." This is à Lapide's commentary, and he goes on: " The words, *gift from God*, may have two meanings; they may mean, first, a state itself: as, marriage, celibacy, or the religious state. These states are a gift of God in the sense that he has established them all by himself or through his Church, and that he offers or gives these states to those who wish to accept them. Thus this gift, *proper* to every one of the faithful, comes partly from God, who instituted the state, and partly from the individual will of the chooser of the state. It is, indeed, true that God sometimes inspires certain individuals with a desire for celibacy, and others with a resolution to marry; as it happens when a queen, by marrying, may have virtuous children, who will do great service to Church and state.*

"But God does not always act in this manner; in a great number of cases he abandons altogether to individual freedom the choice of marriage or celibacy. If such a man is in a particular state, for instance, the marriage state, strictly speaking, it is owing to the free choice which he made of the state. It may, however, be said that the *gift* which is *proper* to him, namely, his state, comes to him from God, but only in the sense that God, who governs all things by a general providence, directs every man through his parents, companions, confessors, masters, and so forth, which results in one embracing marriage, another another state, but all freely; for this entire direction does not interfere with the freedom of man.

"Observe, then, that the apostle might have said that every one has the state of life that he saw fit to choose; but he preferred to say: 'Every one has his proper gift from God,' for he sought to console married people. He feared that some of them might annoy themselves and say: 'The apostle would wish us all to lead a life of celibacy like himself, yet I, unhappy being that I am,—I am married; and it is my own fault that I am deprived of the immense advantages of celibacy, and am cast amid the hardships of marriage.'

---

* We have already remarked,—and we shall have occasion to repeat the remark,—that there are cases wherein persons may be bound to marry, or to become religious.

For, weak and afflicted souls are wont to grow discouraged, when they meet difficulties in their state of life. When they remember that they could easily have escaped these annoyances, they torment themselves to no purpose. In order to do away with these useless regrets, St. Paul tells them that their state is a gift from God, in the sense that we have explained, so that every one may live in peace in his state of life; looking upon it as a benefit confirmed by God, and seeking to sanctify himself in it with joy and thankfulness.

"In the next place, by the words, *gift from God*, which St. Paul applies to the states of the Christian life, we may understand the grace proper to every one of these states. To live in conjugal fidelity, married persons stand in need of grace; virgins need another grace for the practice of virginity: and this grace proper to every state comes formally from God. For, in the supposition that you have chosen a particular state,—let us say celibacy,—God will bestow on you the grace and gift peculiar to that state, in order that, if you wish it, you may lead a holy life in that state. And, indeed, since God has not seen fit to prescribe to every man the state of life that he must accept, and has left us all free in this regard, as well as in many other decisions that we have to come to in this world, the wisdom of his providence demands that, when a man has made a choice, he should not be abandoned, and should receive that measure of divine assistance which is indispensable for a Christian life in the state of his choice. Indeed, God and nature never fail us, in necessary matters especially, because God wills all men to be saved, according to the apostle (1 Tim. ii, 4), in whatever state they may be. He consequently supplies them with all requisite helps for salvation; and, if they are willing to employ this aid, they have it in their power to lead holy lives and attain salvation.

"Understood in this sense, the words of the apostle, 'Every one has his proper gift from God,' mean (unless, in consequence of accidental circumstances, you are bound to embrace some peculiar state*): Choose for yourself the state you please, and God will give you the grace proper and suitable to that state, so that you may lead a holy life in it. This is the view of St. Ambrose, and it is also what the apostle had in his mind, as is plain from the words, 'I would that all men were even as myself'—just as if he had said: 'I have granted marriage to spouses, I have not commanded it, I should even wish that all would practise perfect chastity: but every one has his proper gift, let him use it.' That is, let him who has the grace of the chastity of virgins or of widowhood, take it as a gift from God; let the married man who has received conjugal chastity, and who in his state

---

* It appears to us necessary to insert this restriction in the text of à Lapide. Indeed he himself gives it at the beginning of our lengthy quotation from him.

behaves in conformity with the divine law, accept his grace as a gift from heaven: let this gift be his consolation, and enable him to live in peace. Now from all this it follows, first, that God gives religious, even apostate religious, a gift and grace sufficient for them to live in chastity if they wish; that is, if they pray, if they fast, if they read pious books, if they work, and keep themselves constantly employed.

"It follows, in the second place, that, if one changes his state for a better one, God will give him a higher gift and a greater grace suited to his new state. We must keep in mind that there are various gifts of God. Some come wholly from him. To this class belong, in the natural order, a sound judgment, memory, a fine character; and in the order of grace, all the virtues which God infuses into the soul: as, faith, hope, charity, such as they are given in baptism to a child just born. But there are other gifts of God, which come indeed from him, but need our coöperation for the production of their effect. In this way holy inspirations are gifts from God; so are good works, and the acts of every virtue, gifts from God: because, in order that we may perform them, God bestows on us a prevenient and a coöperating grace, but after such a fashion, however, that he wishes man to perform these acts freely, and have it in his power to do them or to leave them undone. Chastity belongs also to this class of gifts, and it is in this sense that the apostle styles it a **gift of God.***

"With those who have the habit of observing perfect chastity, the gift of chastity is nothing more than this habit itself; but for those who have not this habit, the gift consists in a sufficient interior and exterior help from grace prepared by God for every man, so that every man can be chaste if he uses this help. From the fact that Jesus Christ has given to all the counsel of celibacy, it follows that he has prepared for, and is ready to give to, every man the grace needed to practise it, for he could never counsel what is impossible: and celibacy is impossible for man without the help of divine grace. If he is ready to bestow on every man the grace of virginal chastity, much more is he ready to give conjugal chastity. Every man, therefore, has his proper gift, that is, the grace suited to his state, in the sense that he can obtain it, and that God holds it in readiness; and he can actually have that grace, that is, he may truly be forestalled and helped by that grace in his actions, if he wills to pray seriously and constantly to God for that prepared assistance, and if he will generously coöperate with the grace that God actually gives him." †

This long passage is taken from the learned Cornelius à Lapide; and the doctrine of this illus-

---

* St. Chrysostom understands the words of the apostle in the same way. (*De virginitate*, c. xxxvi.)   † In 1 Cor. c. vii, 7.

trious commentator of the Scriptures appears to flow clearly from the principles which we laid down in the first part of this book. For, since, as we have proved, marriage, celibacy, and the religious life are holy states, and are not in themselves obligatory on the faithful, it is evident that, where there is no hindrance, we are free to choose among these states the one that suits us, when we are not so situated that some one of them becomes obligatory on us through accidental circumstances.

These views receive confirmation from what the fathers of the Church say on the freedom of all men to practise or not to practise virginity. Suarez cites the following text from St. Basil: "At the opening of his career every one is allowed to desire and embrace the kind of life to which he aspires, provided it is a licit kind of life. Every one is free to marry or to lead a life of celibacy."*

Are we to infer from this that, when God does not call a soul to one state more than to another, she may lightly and giddily embrace the state which flatters most the tendencies of nature? By no means. In all his actions man should be guided by reason; and to put this reason aside where there is question of taking a determination on which depends the happiness of a whole life,

---

* Suar., lib. 9, c. ii, n. 5. Cf. St. Chrysost. *de virginitate*, capp. xxxviii, xxxix.

would be the strangest and most fatal blindness. The Christian in all his works must follow the guidance of faith: and is the light of faith ever more necessary to him than in the choice of a state of life? Who does not see that salvation is vastly concerned in such a choice? To give a decisive solution, therefore, to the grave question of vocation, it is important for every one to use every means to learn the state of life in which he can live most agreeably to God, and most beneficially for his own salvation. The rules of Christian prudence should also be observed.

These means and rules shall form the subject-matter of the two following sections. We shall revert briefly to the doctrine and principles heretofore laid down: clearness and precision require us to do so.

SECT. I.—MEANS TO KNOW WHAT STATE OF LIFE WE SHOULD CHOOSE.

These means are all contained in the three words: pray, reflect, consult.

CHAPTER I.

PRAYER.

"Who is the man that can understand his own way?" (Prov. xx, 24.) How can we by ourselves foresee all the dangers that are to be met with in this or that state, even though it be lawful and holy? God alone knows the means and the obstacles that his creature is to find in its path. Man sees the opening of the career, and, as it were, the beginning of the road, that lies before him; but, inexperienced in travel, he knows neither the thorns that will blood-stain his feet, nor the stones against which he may stumble, nor the precipice whose depths shall yawn beneath his steps. What is to be done amid such darkness save to cry out to God with the Royal Prophet: "Enlighten my eyes that I may never sleep in death;"* "O Lord! make me know my end;"† "Teach me to do thy will, for thou art my God. Make the way known to me wherein I should walk; for I have lifted up my soul to thee;"‡ "Turn away my eyes that they may not behold vanity;"§ "Give me understanding"?‖

---

* Ps. xii, 4. † Ps. xxxviii, 5. ‡ Ps. cxlii, 8-10.
§ Ps. cxviii, 37. ‖ Ibid., 73.

When the wind whirling about the sands of the desert hides from the traveller the road that he should follow, his only guide are the stars of heaven. "As we know not what to do, we can only turn our eyes to thee." * "If any of you want wisdom, let him ask of God who giveth to all men abundantly, and upbraideth not; and it shall be given to him." † This wisdom, as Cornelius à Lapide notices, is nothing else but a knowledge of our last end, and of the means to reach it. And who is there that has greater need of this wisdom than young people without experience in life, and still having to choose a state in it? No one more than they has to fear the deceptions and prejudices of the world, the rush of passions and of a fiery imagination, and the fascination of trifles which shroud real good in darkness. Let them pray, therefore. Indeed, if prayer is at all times a consolation, a strength, a light, for the Christian in all his leading actions, is its presence not needed to direct, sustain, and cheer him in the greatest and most decisive step of his life,—the choice of a state? With good reason, then, has every author who deals with this matter recommended prayer,—earnest, ardent prayer, before making such a choice. St. Ignatius says that we should "entreat the mercy of God, that he will vouchsafe to instruct our mind and impel our will in that direction in which we ought in

---

* 2 Paral. xx, 12.   † Jas. i, 5.

preference to go." * "We should pray earnestly to God," wrote St. Liguori to a young man, "to make known to us his will, whatever may be the state he has in store for us."† The chief favor which we ought to beg of God, after our first communion, is, according to us, to know the kind of life in which we shall most easily save our souls. Wherefore it is important from early life to practise some daily devotion or penance, with a view to gain this knowledge. "Do not fail," continues St. Liguori, "to recommend yourself in a special way to our holy mother, the Blessed Virgin Mary, beseeching her to obtain for you grace perfectly to fulfil the will of her divine Son."‡

St. Louis Gonzaga paid frequent visits to our Lady's altar, fasted every Saturday in her honor, and often received holy communion for the same object. On the feast of the Assumption, having eaten the bread of angels, whilst in the name of Mary he besought the Holy Ghost to manifest his will, the young saint learned, in a clear and definite way, what God wished him to do.§ The Blessed Virgin is, indeed, the star that God has made to shine over the ocean of this world to guide unto the haven of salvation the tempest-tost children of men. Turn not away your eyes from the light of that star, if you wish to escape

---

* St. Ign. in lib., *Exerc. modus prior electionis.*
† St. Lig., "Retreat."   ‡ Id. (Ascetic Works.)
§ Rossignoli, "The Choice of a State," c. xi.

the fury of the waves, says St. Bernard. In all your doubts and anxieties think of Mary, call upon her name.*

By invoking God and his holy mother with perseverance, confidence, fervor, docility, and the other necessary conditions, we shall surely obtain, if not a revelation and extraordinary lights on the path we should follow, at least the purity of intention and the Christian prudence which we need to make a choice in accordance with God and with our holy faith. Jesus Christ has promised to grant everything to well-made prayer.† We must not, however, neglect those other means which we have still to mention. Also, let us not forget that, when mortal sin reigns in a soul, it acts like a cloud veiling from us the light of heaven, and hindering the ardor of prayer. "Your iniquities," says Isaias (lix, 2), "have divided between you and your God, and your sins have hid his face from you." "The way of the wicked is darksome: they know not where they fall." (Prov. iv, 19.)

Who can refrain from pitying those young people who grovel in evil thoughts and pursuits up to the hour at which they have come to a final decision on their future? Will some few hastily uttered aspirations, a few returns for a moment to virtue, be able to scatter the clouds

---

* *Homil. Super. Missus est, Brev. Rom. in fest. S. Nom. Mariæ.*
† These are the views of Lessius, q. 6, n. 77.

that have been heaped up by a guilty life? Saul consulted the Lord, and could get no answer: God withdrew from the king who had refused to obey his commands. (1 Kings, xxviii, 6, 18.) Hence, he who wishes to learn what state he should embrace, ought to keep himself constantly in the state of grace by receiving the sacraments, at least often enough to avoid grievous sin. This is what will render prayer efficacious, make it penetrate the heavens, and bring down on the soul the mercy and light of the Almighty.

CHAPTER II.

REFLECTION.

"With desolation is all the land made desolate," says the prophet, "because there is none that considers in his heart." (Jer. xii, 11.) It is this absence of reflection that every day throws into careers not made for them men who are swayed, not by reason or by grace, but by the threefold concupiscence spoken of in St. John. Who can tell the amount of evil which this thoughtlessness begets in individuals, in families, and in society at large? How many beings lead hapless lives because they are out of their true way; into how many dangers for salvation are not souls plunged inconsiderately, which might have been avoided by a little care and foresight! What noble talents are buried in the earth, what grand intellects become utterly powerless! What countless souls, capable of the sublimest achievements, waste away in trifles and folly! "O ye sons of men, how long will you be dull of heart? Why do you love vanity, and seek after lying?" (Ps. iv, 3.) Do you not fear the endless despair of those who shall cry out on the day of wrath, "Therefore we have erred from the way of truth, we fools"? (Wisd. v, 6.) "O that they" (young people) "would be wise and would understand, and would provide for their last end" (Deut. xxxii, 29), in the important affair of the choice of a state of life. "Prudence," says the Angelical Doctor, "is one of the most necessary virtues for human life. To live well is to do well; but to do well, it is not enough to act. We must, besides, act in a proper manner, that is to say, follow a righteous decision, and not be led by mere impulse or passion."* But if this righteous decision is required in all human acts, it is still more needful when there is question of one of the most decisive and important acts of our whole existence on earth. Now, among the faults opposed to prudence, St. Thomas reckons imprudence, precipitation, and thoughtlessness, or want of reflection.† This last defect consists in overlooking or neglecting things that may lead to a wrong judgment, and it is evident that this is a defect.‡

But thinking, or reflection, ought to be used by a man chiefly in important undertakings, and therefore in the choice of a state of life. It is then, above all, that he should meditate carefully on the end of man here below. For, as St. Thomas remarks, to make a right and just choice, we must set before ourselves a proper end: *"Rectitudo electionis requirit debitum finem."*

---

* St. Th., 1, 2, q. 57, a. 5.   † Id., 2, 2, q. 53, a. 2-4.   ‡ Ibid.

In his Exercises,—to which the Holy See has given such direct and laudatory approbation, and whose authority is consequently of the greatest weight,—the illustrious founder of the Society of Jesus says that, in order to choose anything well, it is our duty, with a pure and single eye, to consider for what we were created, namely: for the praise of God, and our own salvation.*

The grand, fundamental, and luminous principle which should direct and enlighten this grave deliberation, is this: "Man was created for this end, that he might praise and reverence the Lord his God, and, serving him, at length be saved. But the other things which are placed on the earth were created for man's sake, that they may assist him in pursuing the end of his creation; whence it follows that they are to be used or abstained from in proportion as they profit or hinder him in pursuing that end." † The letters of St. Liguori, from which we are about to make some quotations, aim at impressing these lofty thoughts on the minds of young men.

To a young man who asked his advice about the kind of life he ought to embrace, the saint wrote: "If you desire to follow the state of life that is the surest to reach salvation, which is for us the all-important point, remember that your soul is immortal, and that the end for which God placed you in this world is, assuredly, not to gain riches

---

* *Prælud. ad elect.* † Ibid., "1ª *hebd. principium.*"

and honors, nor to lead an easy and agreeable life, but solely to merit everlasting life by the practice of virtue. On the day of judgment it will profit you nothing to have shed lustre around your family, nor to have shone in the world: the only thing that will then be of any service to you will be to have loved and served Jesus Christ, who will be your judge. The evil is, that in the world little thought is given to God, and to that other world in which we are to dwell forever. All, or nearly all, the thoughts of men are for the things of earth. As a consequence, life is irksome, and worse than death itself. If, then, you wish to be sure of making a good choice of a state of life, represent yourself as at the point of death, and choose the state which then you will wish to have embraced. Remember that all things here below have an end. Everything passes away, and death advances toward us. At every step we take, we go nearer to death and to eternity. At the moment we think least of it, death will be at our door; and then what comfort shall we find in the goods of this life? Shall we find in them anything more than delusion, vanity, falsehood, and folly? And all that will contribute only to make us end an unhappy life by a still more unhappy death."*

The holy doctor wrote in the same strain to a young lady: "Examine," said he, " what is most

---

* St. Lig., "Answer to a Young Man." (Ascetic Works.)

advantageous for you, what can best make you happy: whether it is to have for spouse a man of this earth, or to have for spouse Jesus Christ, the Son of the King of heaven. See which of these two alliances appears to you the better, and choose it. Consider likewise what may be the consequences of the state that you choose, either in going into the world, or in giving yourself to Jesus Christ. The world offers you the goods of this earth; on the other hand, Jesus Christ holds out to you a cross. That is what he himself preferred while he was in this world. But he unites with it two immense advantages: peace of heart in this life, and heaven in the life to come. Blessed is he who saves his soul; woe to him who damns it. See what has become of so many grand ladies, so many princesses and queens, who in the world were waited on, praised, honored, and all but adored. If they have had the misfortune to lose their souls, what have they now of all their wealth, their pleasures, and their honors? Remorse and torments that shall overwhelm them forever as long as God shall be God, and leave them not a ray of hope ever to retrieve their eternal loss. Hence, my dear daughter, since you have to choose a state in which to spend your whole life, take the one which you would be glad to have taken if you were about to die. Think well on it. In the world there is a vast number of women who damn their souls; the number of those who lose their souls in convents is very small."*

When, by thoughts of this nature, the soul has convinced herself that all is vanity save loving God and serving him alone; when she understands fully her real end, she must, besides, in a sincere election, reflect on the means suited and proper to that end: "*Rectitudo electionis*," says St. Thomas, "*requirit id quod convenienter ordinatur ad debitum finem.*"†

"Those things alone are to be chosen," says St. Ignatius, "which conduce to our end, since in all cases the means ought to be subordinate to the end, not the end to the means. Wherefore they err who determine first to marry a wife, or take an ecclesiastical office or benefice, and then afterward serve God; reversing the use of the end and means, and not going straight to God, but obliquely endeavoring to draw him over to their own perverse desires. The true way to act is the direct contrary: to set before ourselves first the service of God as our end, and then to choose marriage or the priesthood, as well as all other things, so far as it is expedient, they being ordered toward the end previously determined."‡

"But in order to know what state will best suit our end, we must reflect. We must interrogate the experience of our past falls, the causes of our

---

* "Advice to a Young Woman." (Ascetic Works.)
† Ibid., St. Th., 1, 2, q. 57, a. 5. ‡ *Exerc. prælud. electionis.*

sins, the nature of our aptitudes, the excellences, the advantages, the dangers, of the several states of life. We will not enter here into any details. What we have said in the first part of this book, while it gives a correct idea of the different states of the Christian life, will also serve to direct the reflections which every serious mind ought to make. It is true that, while living in the world, it is not always easy to enter into one's self; and hence theologians * and the masters of the spiritual life advise persons who are about to choose a state of life, to spend some days in retreat in the quiet and retirement of a religious house, far from the noise of the world and the bustle of business. Here is what St. Liguori wrote to a young man: "If a spiritual retreat is good for all classes of persons, it is especially useful for any one that wishes to choose properly a state of life. The first object aimed at in the establishment of these pious exercises was the choice of a state." † The holy doctor afterward advised the same young man to read a book of meditation, which would take the place of sermons, and to get the Lives of the Saints. This advice is especially needful for those who cannot enjoy the benefit of a retreat. They should endeavor to make up this deficiency by serious reading, and by studying the examples of the chosen ones of God. Was

---

* Lessius, *De statu vitæ eligendo*, q. 6, n. 77.
† "Retreat." (Ascetic Works.)

it not on hearing read these words of Scripture, "Go, sell all thou hast" (Matt. xix, 21), that St. Anthony and St. Francis of Assisi resolved to enter on a poor and penitential life? Was it not meditation on those other words of our blessed Lord, "What does it profit a man to gain the whole world, if he lose his soul" (Matt. xvi, 26), that opened the eyes of St. Francis Xavier to the vanities of the world and the glory of earth, and of a university professor made an apostle? "Can I not do what others do?" St. Augustine used to exclaim, when thinking of men who led a chaste life; and by putting himself this question, he stimulated himself to return from the wanderings of his early years. Let every one, then, who cannot snatch from his occupations the time necessary to shut himself up in solitude and meditate there, reflect every day while attending to his duties, and study in good books, and in the silence of a recollected soul, the heroism of saints and the glorious thoughts of our faith.

CHAPTER III.

CONSULTATION.

"My son, do nothing without counsel, and thou shalt not repent when thou hast done." (Ecclus. xxxii, 24.) "The Holy Ghost," says à Lapide commenting on these words, "has here in view works that are difficult and of some importance. To undertake them, we need, particularly in youth, to consult prudent men." This is what Tobias recommended to his son: "Seek counsel always of a wise man." (Tobias iv, 19.) Whatever is done according to right and wise counsel is well done, and gives no cause for repentance. If, after having taken advice, we do not succeed, we can solace ourselves with the thought that we did not follow our own views, but abided by those whose counsel it was fitting to take. "Lean not on thine own prudence," says the Holy Ghost. (Prov. iii, 5.) "Woe to you that are wise in your own eyes, and prudent in your own conceits." (Isa. v, 21.) It is very much to be feared that this malediction falls on those who without advice rashly take upon themselves the responsibility of choosing a state of life.

As it is of the highest importance to take advice before coming to any irrevocable decision, so it is equally important not to select bad counsellors. " Advise not with fools, for they cannot love but such things as please them." (Ecclus. viii, 20.) On this text the learned à Lapide again says: " The foolish and the wicked counsel what is in the line of their passions and interests, not what is profitable to others. We must not, therefore, apply to men who do not fear God as they should. ' Treat not with a man without religion concerning holiness, nor with an unjust man concerning justice.' (Ecclus. xxxvii, 12.) ' Consult not with him that layeth a snare for thee.' (Ibid. 7.) ' Let one of a thousand be thy counsellor.' (Ibid. vi, 6.) ' The same distinguished commentator speaks thus on this passage: " We should consult only a few rare and choice men; for there are not many prudent, few have experience, and fewer still are discreet and faithful."* But it is chiefly when we aspire to a perfect life, that we should avoid a multitude of counsellors. Were we to take the advice of many, who does not see what difficulties would arise? Because carnal men, who are always in the majority, hinder rather than promote the desire of perfection, as St. Thomas observes.† " Choose, then, as advisers only such as are prudent and well-minded," adds St. Bernard. " In the vast crowd of mankind it is hard for every

---

* Corn. in hoc, cap. vi.   † Opusc. 17, c. i.

one to find even one man uniting these two qualities in a high degree. It is no easy matter to meet a love of what is really good in a prudent man, or prudence in a man fond of good. The number of those who possess neither quality is very great."* St. Ambrose speaks in similar terms: " When you ask advice," says he, " you should go to a man noted for the probity of his life, for his virtues, for an unflinching love of good, and for the great moderation of his conduct. Who goes to seek a spring of clear water in a puddle, or drinks dirty water? In like manner, who expects to draw anything useful from the confusion of vice? Can a man who does not know how to order his own life, regulate the life of another? How can I consider as my superior in prudence a man whom I see so far below me in his morals? Can I look upon as able to give me counsel, one who is unable to counsel himself? Or am I to suppose that he who neglects his own interests, will take care of mine?"†

" Be continually with a holy man, whomsoever thou shalt know to observe the fear of God; whose soul is according to thine own soul, and who, when thou shalt stumble in the dark, will be sorry for thee." (Ecclus. xxxvii, 15, 16.) This faithful counsellor is a man of God, an enlightened confessor, to whom you disclose your faults, all your evil tendencies, the dangers through which

---

* Apud Corn. in Ecclus. viii, 20.   † Amb., *Offic.*, lib. 2, c. xii.

you have passed, and those which you apprehend in the future. A general confession that will lay before him the wounds and secrets of your soul, will help him in giving salutary advice. It is chiefly for the religious vocation that Suarez requires us to have recourse to counsellors who are virtuous, free from all human ties to the one that consults them, and who have right and correct ideas about a holy and religious life: "*Probi et liberi ab omni humano affectu, quique de vita sancta et religiosa recte sentiant.*" * Therefore these counsellors should not forget that, in the state of perfection, there are, as St. Thomas and Suarez teach, fewer occasions of sin, more abundant means of salvation, and facility for perseverance in grace; that, in order to enter that state, there is no necessity of a previously virtuous life, since it is suited to repentant sinners, and even to those who have recently embraced the faith.† " Among the things chiefly to be attended to in taking advice upon entrance into religion" (it is still Suarez who speaks), "the first is to consult those who can help, instead of hindering, our purpose: '*Ab his petatur qui possunt prodesse et non obesse.*' Furthermore, it is judicious to consult, as far as possible, men who have some experimental knowledge of the religious state: '*et, si fieri possit, aliquod experimentum illius habeant.*' The second point to be attended to is, that the consultation be

---

* Suar., lib. 5, c. viii, n. 2. † Div. Th., opusc. 17.

prudent and serious indeed, as the grave nature of the subject requires it to be; but not too protracted. Long delays are not necessary: often they are an obstacle to a divine vocation, and the source of a multitude of dangers." *

When there is question of entering the married state, we should, as the catechism of the Council of Trent bids, zealously exhort children to "pay it as a tribute of respect due to their parents, or to those under whose guardianship and authority they are placed, not to engage in marriage without their knowledge, still less in defiance of their express wishes." †

"Father Pinamonti says with good reason," observes St. Liguori, "that, to choose the religious state, it is neither necessary nor proper that children should await the counsel of their parents, not only because these latter have no experience on the subject, but also because, blinded by self-interest, they turn into enemies."‡ We do not wish to repeat here what we spoke of at so much length in the first part of this work.§ Yet we cannot leave unnoticed the comment of à Lapide on the words of the Holy Ghost, that we have cited. Here it is: "They go against the rules of prudence given them by Holy Writ, who, being called to serve God and to do him honor in the religious state, take counsel of seculars, of

---

* Suar., lib. 5, c. viii, n. 2. † *De matrim.*, n. 37.
‡ St. Lig., *Theol. Mor.*, lib. 4, n. 68. § Sect. 2, c. xi.

relatives, or of parents. St. Bernard cries out eloquently on this subject: 'How many lose a vocation through the accursed influence of worldly wisdom, which quenches in them the holy fire that God sought to kindle in their hearts! This treacherous wisdom says: Be very much on your guard against over-haste; reflect long on the matter; look prudently into everything. You set before yourself a great undertaking: you should think much on it. Try your strength, consult your friends, so that, later, you may never have reason to repent of your step.' This wisdom of the world is earthy, animal, diabolical, the enemy of salvation. It chokes life and breeds lukewarmness. Be careful, it tells you. And why would you be careful? When the Angel of the great counsel calls, what need have you to wait for other counsels? Let him consult his friends who has not heard these words of Christ: 'A man's enemies shall be they of his own household.' (Matt. x, 36.) Why does he profess to believe the Gospel who does not obey it?"*

Lessius, speaking as a theologian, is not less explicit. "The fathers of the Church," he says, "have always been of opinion that, to be enlightened on vocation, we must never seek advice from men of the world. Dazzled by the false glitter of earthly things, they do not know the worth of invisible goods. In their eyes voluntary

---

* See à Lapide on Ecclus. xxxvii, 12.

poverty is a wretched state, they look on chastity as an effect of a sour temper, and they hold obedience to be a mere slavery. A simple and coarse dress is for them contemptible, a convent is a prison, and all the exercises of a religious life pass for a silly occupation. On the other hand, they make the greatest account of wealth, honors, and splendid marriages. Now, it is impossible that men over whom the world has so much sway should inspire with holy resolves those who seek their advice about the religious life: for every one judges and counsels according to his peculiar views."[*]

SECT. II.—RULES TO BE FOLLOWED IN CHOOSING A STATE OF LIFE.

These rules, which are borrowed from theology and the most eminent masters of the spiritual life, will, we trust, be useful, not only to persons deliberating on the state they should embrace, but to those also who are called upon to advise and direct them in this deliberation.

---
[*] Lessius, q. 4, n. 38.

CHAPTER I.

RULES TO BE FOLLOWED WHEN A STATE IS OBLI-GATORY.

WE have proved in the first part that marriage, celibacy, and the religious life, are not in themselves binding under precept. That is to say, apart from exceptional cases, no man is obliged, by any commandment of God, to enter one of these states rather than another. There are, however, circumstances which may make a state obligatory for this or that person. It is clear that one who happens to be in such a case has no necessity of long deliberation to discover his state, since it is made known to him by some precept. For him it is a duty of conscience to follow that state. Now, here are the chief cases in which a state becomes obligatory.

In the first place, he who would have no other means than marriage to hinder some great calamity, such as a great war, political convulsions, and other dangers of the same kind; or, again, who would have no other means than marriage to restore the true religion to a large country, would be bound to marry. Suarez and à Lapide, who state this case, say that it is of rare occurrence.*

In the next place, he who is bound neither by vow of chastity, nor by vow to enter religion, yet lives a disorderly life, and will use no other means save marriage to amend his life, is bound to embrace that state.† Indeed, if, in entering that state, he were not resolved to respect its sacred laws, it would not help him to live in a Christian manner. Supposing, however, the intention to comply with all the duties of the state, marriage should be counselled to any one who is in either of the above cases.‡

We have already stated that the obligation of marriage does not hold for him who is willing to employ other means for the preservation of chastity. "Who has ever pretended," asks St. Liguori, "that marriage is indispensable in order to keep out of sin? The words of St. Paul, 'If they do not contain themselves, let them marry' (1 Cor. vii, 9), apply to those only who will use no other means to triumph over temptation. This is the meaning generally attached to these words by the interpreters of Holy Scripture." §

Virginity, celibacy, and widowhood are likewise obligatory forever, when they have been vowed forever. After such vows it would be a grievous sin to get married, unless dispensed for

---

* Suar., *De voto cast.*, lib. 9, c. ii, n. 7.   † Lig., lib. 3, n. 209.
‡ See Part I, Art. I, c. ii.   § *Theol. Mor.*, lib. 6, n. 75.

just reasons; but it is plain that such vows are no hindrance to entering religion.

The religious life also becomes obligatory for those who have vowed it to God, if they took that vow after having reached the use of reason.

We have before cited the following passage from St. Liguori's Theology: " Were any one in the belief that, by remaining in the world, he would lose his soul, either because he has already had sad experience of his own weakness amid the dangers of the world, or because he has not those aids which the religious life supplies, he could not be excused from grave sin if he remained in the world, since he thereby would expose himself to imminent danger of being eternally lost."*

The number of persons in this case is, perhaps, far greater than is imagined. "The Emperor Mauritius having issued an edict which forbade soldiers to become monks, St. Gregory the Great wrote to him that the law was unjust, because it closed heaven on many souls. Here are the words and reasons of that pope: ' There are very many who cannot save their souls unless they renounce all things: *Nam plerique sunt qui, nisi omnia reliquerint, salvari apud Deum nullatenus possunt.*' " † Lessius, quoted by St. Liguori, says: " If your conscience tells you, as it often happens, that God will abandon you unless you obey his

---

* *Theol. Mor.*, lib. 4, n. 78.   † Ibid.

divine call, that you will be lost if you remain in the world, it is a sin for you not to follow that call." St. Liguori ends by saying that persons called to religion are bound to follow it: "*De vocatis dico teneri.*" He also insists on the dangers incurred when the divine call is disobeyed, and he prays God to ward off such an evil.* This should suffice to determine all whom God calls to a perfect life, to be docile to the inspirations of grace.

But when is one called to the religious state? St. Liguori will answer; and his doctrine will enlighten such as wait almost for a revelation from heaven in order to decide a vocation. According, then, to the holy doctor, the following are the three chief signs of a real vocation:—

First, a good object or intention, such as to retire from the dangers of the world, to make salvation more secure, to attach one's self more closely to God.

Secondly, no positive impediment, such as want of health or talent, parents in great need, and so forth. Everything of this nature is to be submitted to superiors; and the full truth should be told them, in order that they may decide properly for the order and for the applicant.

Thirdly, acceptance by the superiors of the order to which application is made.†

---

* *Theol. Mor.*, lib. 4, n. 78.
† "The Choice of a State." (Ascetic Works, ed. Castermann.) Note by the translator, drawn from "Advice to Novices."

RULES WHEN A STATE IS OBLIGATORY.

When a person has all these conditions, he can go on safely. "It is clear," says Lessius, "that, if the motive which prompts you to enter religion is simply your own spiritual advantage,—thus, for instance, if you become a religious to shun the world's dangers, to imitate the life of Christ, to follow his counsels, to give yourself to God, to serve him more faithfully, to take care of your salvation, and to bring others to do the same,— your vocation evidently comes from God." *

In the conduct of life, it is neither necessary nor proper to await absolute certainty before acting, as the same Lessius observes, according to Bishop Lucquet. Here is a portion of that notable quotation: "When one feels an inclination to give up the world, and imitate the humility of Jesus Christ in the religious state, he is as surely moved to that by the Holy Ghost, as he is surely being moved by the same Spirit of God when he feels an inclination to believe in Jesus Christ, to do penance, to give alms, or undertake any other good work. Nay more, he has the same certainty as for the act of faith that is necessary for salvation."†

Therefore, whenever we have to advise souls that wish to enter religion for a good purpose, we should strengthen them in their holy desire. To thwart or destroy it would be a crime, as

---

* Lessius, q. 5, n. 57.
† Id., q. 3, n. 70; Lucquet, *De la vocation*, t. 2.

St. Liguori teaches. Here are the words which he addresses to directors of consciences: "If the intention of him who wishes to enter the religious life is right, and if he is under no impediment, neither his confessor nor any one else can, without grievous sin, prevent or divert the penitent from following his vocation."*

---

* *Praxis confess.*, n. 92.

CHAPTER II.

RULES WHEN THE RELIGIOUS VOCATION IS DOUBTFUL.

It often happens that aspirants to the religious state do not present the three conditions enumerated by St. Liguori as signs of a real vocation. Now, according to the same doctor, it is vocation that entails obligation to enter religion, as we have said above: *De vocatis dico teneri;* and as those who feel no liking for the state are not bound to enter it, * unless they have vowed it, or that their salvation is, to a certain extent, impossible in the world,—where the vocation is not clear, the obligation to follow it is uncertain. Here is the case put by Suarez: "Sometimes a person, having neither leaning to nor desire of the religious state, experiences, however, certain thoughts and impressions from grace with respect to the dangers of the world, the excellence and advantages of the religious life, the importance of the choice of a state, and the indifference in which one should be, so as to seek in that choice only the holy will of God. In this

---

* Theol. mor. lib. 4. n. 78.

case, according to the ordinary manner of judging and speaking, one is not supposed to have a religious vocation, even where these thoughts and motives are the beginning of a call from the Holy Ghost. In such circumstances it is not rash to think of the religious state, or to take advice about it. To warrant the taking of advice, some incipient good thoughts on the religious life, inspired by grace, are sufficient: *Loquendo prædicto vulgari modo, negandum est esse temerarium, sine vocatione Spiritus Sancti, de religionis ingressu tractare aut consultare.*

"It is reasonable to consult another to learn whether it be right to enter religion without a supernatural inclination, or without a special desire for the religious life, but solely from an efficacious choice of that state made after deliberation with ourselves, and advice from others. That a choice so made suffices, and that it is often useful to enter religion through that only influence, is proved by reason and experience. When other works of virtue are in question, it is frequently proper, or rather necessary, to act in this manner. So is it also with reference to entering religion; for there is no reason to await an extraordinary grace, to expect such a call from the Holy Ghost as will give an efficacious desire of the religious life before we take counsel. We must hasten to draw profit from every occasion, from every holy thought, at least to reflect and seek judicious advice." * We have thus seen the line of conduct to be followed when there is only a germ of religious vocation. Counsel should then be taken; and we have heretofore said *from whom* it is to be sought. " We should immediately correspond," says St. Liguori, borrowing the words of St. Francis of Sales, "and cultivate the first motions of the Holy Spirit."†

Let us here inquire: *How is he to act who is consulted in a doubt of this kind?* Suarez replies: " The truth must be told openly to the one who asks advice. He whom the Spirit begins to move, must be helped, either to make him remain firm in his purpose, or to prevent him from resisting grace, and to induce him to merit, by prayers and other good works, more abundant graces."‡ This should be the conduct especially of ministers of the Lord, who are God's coadjutors. (1 Cor. iii, 9.)

Is it allowable, under pretext of trying their vocation, to keep languishing for a long time in the world souls that begin to desire to abandon it? Lessius says: " In this matter no more pernicious counsel could be given. What can be more opposed to right reason and to real prudence than to seek in so dangerous a way to know what in another way can be known more surely, and without any danger at all? The world is not the place to

---

* Suar., lib. 5, c. viii, n. 5.
† Ascetic Works, vol. 3, p. 413, ed. Castermann.
‡ Suar., ibid., n. 10.

remain in order to test one's self. Fly as quickly as possible to some secure asylum." *

Should we view as doubtful the vocation of persons who, on account of the deceptions and misfortunes of life in the world, resolve to enter religion? To throw light on this question, we first admit, with Suarez and St. Liguori, that the most essential condition for a religious vocation is a right intention. "This disposition," says Suarez, "is required for every good, and therefore still more so for a work of such grave importance. Hence they deceive themselves who become religious on account of family troubles, and the hardships which they endure, or to escape poverty and contempt. Motives of this kind are not good, or at least they are not so good as the holiness of the religious state requires motives to be." †

St. Liguori has told us that "an intention is right or pure when we purpose to shun the dangers of the world, to make our salvation safer, and to unite ourselves more closely to God."‡ "However, we must not," says Suarez, "confound an intention with the occasion which prompts it. For, frequently, the desire to enter religion springs up in the soul on the occasion of some temporal misfortune, while afterward the motive which decides us to put this desire into execution is not the temporal misfortune, but the will to

---

* Lucquet, vol. 2, pp. 312-314 ; Lessius, q. 7, n. 81.
† Suar., lib. 5, c. viii, n. 6.
‡ Ascetic Works, vol. 3, ed. Castermann.

serve God. At times some failure, some sorrow, leads us to think on eternal goods, to despise everything transitory; and thus a man comes, little by little, to wish to seek after the things of heaven, and renounce all that is earthly. Therefore we should be slow to think lightly of the tendencies of a soul to the religious life, even when they arise on the occasion of temporal evils. It is then that these aspirations should be studied with greater attention. When a misfortune is only the occasion of a desire for a perfect life, it is no obstacle to a divine vocation. It is rather a means which God uses often to draw us to the practice of his counsels."*

"God," says St. Liguori, quoting St. Francis of Sales, "has many ways to call his servants. Sometimes he makes use of sermons; at others, of the reading of good books. Some were called by hearing passages of the Gospel read, as St. Francis of Assisi and St. Antony the Hermit; others, through the disgust, calamities, and afflictions which they experienced in the world, and which led them to fly from it. Although these latter come to God in bad humor with the world, they still withal give themselves to him freely and generously; and such persons often rise to greater holiness than those who entered the service of God with more apparent vocations. Platus relates that a gentleman dressed in the height of fashion, one

---

* Suar., lib. 5, c. viii, nn. 6, 7.

day, did all in his power, when mounted on a superb steed, to win the admiration of some ladies who were near him. On a sudden, the animal threw him into the mud, and the poor man got up in a sorry plight. He was so much ashamed and confused at the accident he had met with, that he fell into a violent passion, and resolved on the spot to become a religious. He asked admission into an order, was received, and led a very holy life.*

Even when secondary views, such as hope of temporal advantages, are connected with the supernatural motive, the vocation is still to be accepted. For, among other advantages, the religious state also comprises temporal good: and this good can be taken into account, provided it is neither the chief nor the only motive that sways us to enter religion. The gold dug up from the mine is none the less gold because some earth clings to it; † so, a religious vocation does not cease to be true, though linked in a secondary way with some human motives. Here several questions present themselves for solution.

First: *Do dissatisfaction and inconstancy in the desire for a religious life always make a vocation doubtful?*

"For a proof of a real vocation," says St. Francis of Sales, "a sensible constancy is not requisite;

---

* St. Francis of Sales cited by St. Liguori. (Ascetic Works, ed. Castermann, vol. 3, p. 413.)

† Pinamonti, "Victorious Vocation," c. iii; Lessius, q. 3, nn. 64, 67.

it is enough that one be firm in mind. We must not therefore judge that a person is not really called because he happens, even before leaving the world, no longer to experience the sensible emotions which he felt in the beginning; nor even because dislikes and coldnesses arise in him which make him waver and suppose that all hope is at an end. It is enough that the will remain constant and not abandon the holy vocation; or even that he continue to entertain some attachment for it."* "Should the pious desires of a young man slacken for a time, that may still be a proof of vocation," says Father Pinamonti. "For, why did he grow cold? Why has he neglected prayer and the sacraments? Why has he allowed his soul to be stained with mortal sin? All these reasons go to prove that the inspiration came from God, since it is strengthened by good works and weakened by evil deeds. Sins and falls are of great assistance in teaching us the nature of divine inspirations, even while they trouble them, and seem to interrupt their course."†

"People of the world are wrong when they think that want of perseverance in holy desires is an evident sign that these desires were ill-founded. It is not thus that the masters of the spiritual life reason. 'The works of God,' says St. Thomas, in relation to this subject, 'are not unalterable,'‡ and

---

* St. Lig., ibid., p. 413. † Pinamonti, "Victorious Vocation," c. iii.
‡ St. Th., 2, 2, q. 189, a. 10.

it would be heresy to assert that we cannot forfeit the grace which we have received."*

Can it be straightway said that a man is unfit for the religious state, because he has for some time led a life of sin, or still feels strong inclinations to sin? As we have already seen, St. Thomas teaches that the religious state is suited for sinners who return to God. Experience, too, shows that, with good will and God's grace, men, very prone to anger or to other passions, have learned to practise all the virtues of religion in full perfection. Such men are bound in the world to avoid the defects to which their corrupt nature impels them: now, is it evident that they can triumph more readily amid the dangers of the world than in the religious life? We must keep in mind the saying of a theologian cited by Suarez,—a saying that deserves to be noted as Suarez himself says, *sententia notanda.* It is this: " Every one should consider the religious state as suited to him, unless he has acquired a certainty of the contrary, either from solid reasons or from experience."†

"When any one enters religion, we are bound," says St. Thomas, "to presume that he is led by the spirit of God. To put a good interpretation on men's actions, is angelical; to put a bad one, is diabolical. ‡ Besides, let us not forget that the decisive trial of a vocation is the noviceship

---

* Pinamonti, "Victorious Vocation," c. ii.
† Suar., lib. 5, c. viii, n. 2.   ‡ *De Erudit. Princip.*, lib. 5, c. xxx.

prescribed by the laws of the Church. This method of testing a vocation is the best, and it is amply sufficient, as Lessius observes. It keeps away, as much as possible, all occasions and causes of temptation. It also furnishes every means that can protect and develop the precious seed. But, in trying a vocation amid the seductions of the world, the very contrary often takes place."*
"Why would you," adds Lessius, "remain among the obstacles and dangers of the world? What have you to gain there? Knowledge of the world and of its vanities. But, in general, it is hurtful to acquire such experience."† Is it necessary to know evil in order to do good?

Speaking of those who rejoice within themselves, and boast before others, of having been so prudent in allowing persons to enter novitiates that none whom they sent ever left afterward, Bishop Lucquet says that they pride themselves on what ought to be for their conscience a serious cause of fear before God; ‡ because they have required what the Church does not require. Some, who are really called by God, have trouble enough from interior combats, without having to contend with external pressure. Indeed, to follow the counsels of Christ, many are far more in need of encouragement than of trial.§

In regard to those upon whom it devolves to

---

* Lessius, q. 7, n. 84.
† *De la vocation*, vol. 2, p. 299.
‡ Ibid., q. 2, n. 22.
§ Ibid., p. 316.

receive persons into religion, they should follow the rules of prudence, and never receive only those who are fit for the religious life, who are called by God, and who have the qualities necessary for the order to which they aspire. The superior of a religious house or order is bound to follow these rules: it is a duty of his office, and it is also a duty of charity, in reference to the one seeking admission. Before admitting any one, therefore, superiors should examine and test him sufficiently so as to be able to pass a prudent judgment on his qualifications. But in what is this test or trial to consist? That is to be left to the decision of a prudent man.* Besides this, in admitting subjects into religion, the rules of the various orders should always be kept in view.† Let us here reply, with Suarez, to the following question: *Is he who, in any religious order, has power to receive subjects, bound to admit a postulant that possesses all the requisite qualifications?*

The learned theologian says that he is bound by duty and by charity, unless he has some reasonable cause for refusing admission. To reject a candidate without good reason, would be to deprive religion of a member, and to shut out a soul from a great good in which the children of the Church can share. Hence St. Basil says: "When Jesus in the words, 'Come to me all you that labor and are burdened' (Matt. xii, 28),

---

* Suar., lib. 5, c. 10, n. 23. † Ibid., n. 27.

invites men, it is dangerous that those who wish to approach the Lord through us, should be driven away by us."

"However," says the same theologian, "this obligation is not so pressing for superiors that it cannot cease from various causes, such as, for instance, the inability of a house to support a new subject. Were several of equal merit to ask admission at the same time, some of them might be accepted and others refused, even though called to the religious life. Finally, in a doubt as to whether a postulant has the required qualifications or not, he may be rejected."* It is, however, to be remembered that a candidate need not be perfect before his admission into the religious state, because it is a state of perfection to be acquired, not of already acquired perfection. All that is necessary for religious profession is a sincere will to tend to perfection. In erring on this point, a community might secure greater peace for itself from the fact that it would mercilessly close its doors against certain troublesome characters. But is no account to be taken of the dangers that abound in the world; and is no fear to be had of throwing among its rocks and shoals a poor soul that yearns after the haven of religion?

"Let a young woman be as hard to deal with as you please," writes St. Francis of Sales, "if in her chief actions she is moved by grace, and not

---

* Suar., lib. 5, c. x, n. 28.

by nature, according to grace and not according to nature she deserves to be accepted, with lov and respect, as the temple of the Holy Ghost: though she is a wolf in nature, she is a lamb by grace. I do not think that monasteries ought to send away all repentant girls. Prudence must be moderated by sweetness, and sweetness or gentleness by prudence. At times so much is to be got from repentant souls, that nothing should be refused them." *

---

* Letters 598 and 600 cited by Bishop Lucquet, "Vocation," vol. 2, p. 342.

CHAPTER III.

RULES WHEN THOSE WHO ARE ABOUT TO CHOOSE A STATE HAVE NOT EVEN A DOUBTFUL VOCATION FOR THE RELIGIOUS LIFE.

THERE are souls which are not in the case of persons for whom marriage, or virginity, or the religious life, is obligatory; and still they feel no desire, they have not even an idea, of the advantages to be met with in the state of perfection. At the same time they are not wanting in the requisites for any state of the Christian life. How should these persons act?

First, they cannot enter that state with regard to which they labor under impediments. For instance, they cannot enter religion if their parents are in extreme need of them.

Secondly, as a right intention is requisite for every good act,* it is especially so for the choice of a state of life.

Thirdly, " Man," says St. Liguori, " is bound to refer all his actions to God, whenever he acts deliberately and for a purpose. For St. Paul writes: ' Whether you eat, or drink, or whatsoever else

---

* Suar., lib. 5, c. viii, n. 6.

you do, do all to the glory of God.' (1 Cor. x, 31.) If, then, a man refers his acts, and, consequently, his choice of a state of life, to God, with a virtual intention, these acts will be good; and they will be bad, if not referred to God."*

To become meritorious, according to a distinguished theologian, an act must be referred to God considered as the author of the supernatural order.† But if a young man who is under no obligation from accidental causes to follow a particular state, and who feels no supernatural leaning for the state of perfection, has a right intention, and refers to God the choice which he is about to make of some state belonging to the Christian life, he falls evidently under the case spoken of by à Lapide when he says: "God leaves many entirely free to choose their state of life: *In multorum arbitrio omnino relinquit ut eligant vel matrimonium vel cælibatum.*" ‡

This follows from all that we have said. This young man is not bound to enter religion, since we suppose him not to have even the beginning of a vocation, and that his salvation is not morally impossible in the world. Nor is he bound to observe celibacy or to get married, since we suppose him not to be in any of those circumstances which render celibacy or marriage obligatory. Besides marriage, celibacy and the religious state are open

---

* St. Lig., *Theol. Mor.*, lib. 2, n. 44.
† Perrone, *De gratia*, part 3, c. iii.   ‡ Comment. in 1 Cor. vii, 7.

to him, because, in our supposition, there are no impediments in his way, and he has all the aptitudes required by every one of these states. If, then, after having prayed, reflected, and consulted, he freely chooses one among these several states, taking care meanwhile to refer his choice to God, to have a right intention, and a will always to fulfil his duties, his choice will be a good one, and even meritorious, when the young man is in the state of grace. Should he marry, he will do well. " If thou take a wife, thou hast not sinned," says St. Paul. " He that giveth his virgin in marriage does well." (1 Cor. vii, 28, 38.) Recall here the lawful ends to be kept in view in entering the marriage state: we enumerated them, Part I, Art. I, c. iv.

But let us advance a step further. He who would unjustly seek to prevent the above-mentioned young man from marrying, would be guilty of a grievous sin;* for he would rob him of a liberty given by God, and divert him from a holy state to which he has a right. But it would not be against any virtue—nay, it would even be a laudable act, to tell that same young man, with St. Paul, that virginity is better than marriage. Celibacy is a counsel: it may therefore be counselled in this case under consideration. Much more may the religious life be counselled, since, even when engaged to be married, one has still a

---

* St. Lig., *Theol. Mor.*, lib. 4, n. 335. Ed. Meiller.

right to enter, and because it is still more perfect than celibacy. There is no need here to go into any proof of these propositions: we gave ample demonstration of them in the First Part. St. Ignatius says that out of the Exercises "it is lawful, and to be accounted meritorious, to persuade all those to embrace celibacy, religious life, and any other evangelical perfection, who, from the consideration of their persons and conditions, will probably be fit subjects."* Where a man is free to choose the state which he considers suitable for him, he who seeks most purely to please God will assuredly receive the greatest graces. Hence, in accordance with the Exercises of St. Ignatius, and the Directory that accompanies them, we shall proceed to lay down rules calculated to make the choice of a state in the Christian life as perfect as possible.

---

* S. Ign., 15th Annot., "Book of Exercises."

CHAPTER IV.

RULES TO DISCOVER WHAT IS MOST PLEASING TO GOD, WHEN A PERSON IS FREE TO CHOOSE THE STATE WHICH HE THINKS PROPER FOR HIMSELF.

The question to be met in the choice of a state of life is this: Must I confine myself to the commandments, or must I undertake the practice of the counsels? If I choose the counsels, shall I practise them in the world or in the religious state?*

In order to answer this question, it is important that he who is about to make his choice should be free from every disorderly inclination, and be completely indifferent to everything; having no other tendency than to follow the divine will, whatever it may be, as soon as it shall make itself known. To have a strong leaning toward riches, and little inclination for poverty, would not be a good disposition, and there would be no reason to expect much good from an election made in such a frame of mind. For, any inclination leading the soul away from the most perfect path, and drawing her to one less perfect, would impel the intellect to seek motives to

---
* *Direct.*, c. xxv, nn. 2, 3.

strengthen still more this inclination, and the deliberation would issue in the soul's taking her own will for the will of God.*

Many go wrong, says our illustrious guide, and take as a divine call what is only a badly made choice. A divine call is always pure, clear, and free from carnal affection and perverse desire.† Therefore, he who is about to choose must have reached, by meditation on the example of our Lord and of his saints, such a state of indifference, as to be equally disposed to practise both counsels and commandments, or the commandments only, if such be the divine will.‡

St. Liguori speaks in the same way: "He who is not in this indifference, and still prays to God to enlighten him on the choice of a state of life, and who, instead of conforming to God's will, rather asks God to conform to him, resembles a pilot that pretends to wish his vessel to advance, yet in reality does not want it to stir: he first throws out his anchor, and then unfurls his sails. God does not shed his light on souls thus disposed. On the other hand, if he prays to God with generous indifference, and a resolution to follow his holy will, God will show him clearly what state is best for him."§

Indeed, the best disposition for the choice of a state is not to be as ready to follow the counsels

---

* *Direct.*, c. xxiii, n. 3. † *Introduct. ad eligend. Tertium.*
‡ Ibid., n. 3. § Ascetic Works: "Retreat—To a Young Man."

as the commandments, but even to be more inclined to what is most perfect.* "It is to be observed," says St. Ignatius, "that, when we perceive that our affections are opposed to perfect poverty, which consists in detachment from, and readiness to quit, all things, and that they rather incline to riches, it is very profitable, in order to rid ourselves of such affections, to ask God, even though the flesh resist, that he would call us to poverty. Meanwhile, we should preserve our will free, so that we may in the end go the way which is the more suitable for the service of God."† And truly, even though one were not to choose the state of perfection, because, perhaps, he is not called to it, this perfect disposition not only can do no harm, but must prove even very beneficial to the soul. Hence, during the spiritual exercises, the most perfect way is set before men as one that should be desired and asked of God. In this connection we call attention to the following saying of St. Ignatius, which is found in one of his writings: "He who directs another during a retreat, must so dispose him as to make him as ready to follow the counsels as the commandments. Indeed, then, we should have, as far as depends on us, greater readiness for the counsels, where the observance of them will contribute more to the glory of God. For, more evident tokens are required to decide that God

---

* *Director.*, c. xxiii, n. 4.   † "Exercise on the Three Classes."

wishes a soul to remain in the state of the commandments alone, than to believe that soul called to follow the path of the counsels; for our Lord has very clearly exhorted men to embrace the counsels." *

These grave principles apply chiefly, it seems to us, to persons who have received from heaven more than ordinary talents. "Much shall be asked from him who has received much" (Luc. xii, 48), says our Lord. What we have received is not to be buried in the earth: now, St. Gregory tells us that we bury our talents when we devote them solely to earthly objects: *Talentum abscondere est acceptum ingenium terrenis actibus implicare.* (Hom. ix, in Evang.) In order to foster in the soul a disposition to embrace what is most perfect, we must be careful to meditate on the life of Christ; for, without such meditation, we will not make a good choice of a state of life, and will only hurt ourselves. Meditation strengthens the soul; it enlightens it, lifts it above the earth, makes it fitter to know and do God's will, and to beat down every obstacle. The soul that gives up meditation is weak and in darkness.† " Lastly, let him who is choosing a state remain in deep recollection during his deliberations. Let him close the gates of his senses, and banish from his mind every other thought. Let him give no ear to any other voice than that of heaven. This

---

* *Director.*, c. xxiii, n. 4. † Ibid., c. xxx, n. 3.

means, first, that the soul should not allow itself to be distracted; that it should bury itself only with its election, attend to it alone, and put aside every other interest. Secondly, it means that, during this deliberation, the soul should consider only heavenly motives; that is, it should reject all reasons suggested by flesh and blood, and should not permit itself to be influenced by any human and earthly consideration. Every thought must start from and be based solely on this principle: the desire to glorify God and to do his holy will. This gives the soul great confidence that God will not allow her to be deceived. For, since she seeks him sincerely and with all her heart, he will never turn away from her, because his goodness is too great, and his love for his creatures is so boundless, that he often goes to meet those who flee from his face. Yet, though the choice is excellent when made out of love for God, nevertheless, if, as we already stated, any other motive combines to bend the soul in the same direction, the choice is not ill-made on that account, provided this secondary motive is not in opposition with faith or the divine will, and that it is good in itself; as, for instance, one's own consolation, quiet of mind, health, or some similar incentive. But this latter motive must not be the chief one, nor chiefly influence our decision; and, besides, it must be subordinated to the love of God."*

* *Director.*, c. xxiii, n. 5.

CHAPTER V.

THREE TIMES SUITABLE FOR MAKING A RIGHT CHOICE.

St. Ignatius points out the three states in which a soul may be, and in which she is properly disposed to make a choice conformable to God's will. The first state is when the action of God so influences the human will that it puts an end to all hesitation, and even to the power of hesitating, as to the doing of that to which it impels. This was the case of St. Paul, St. Matthew, and others, whom our Lord called to follow him.* Though, in our days, we witness no vocations exactly of this kind, still there are many that resemble them. In these, the light and consolation shed over the soul are so intense, that all doubt vanishes about the will of God. However, such vocations are extraordinary: no rules can be given respecting them. We should neither ask for them, nor expect them from God.†

A second time favorable for a right election is when the soul is under the influence of inspirations and interior motions so powerful, that,

---

* "Exercise on the Three Times."   † *Director.*, c. xxvi, n. i.

almost without any reasoning of the intellect, the will is borne on toward God and the practice of perfection. This state of a soul is more usual than the first.* Although the intellect and will are so united in us that the one can make no choice without the assistance of the other, however, in the two states of the soul that have just been mentioned, the will precedes, and the intellect follows, carried away without reasoning and without hesitation in the direction of the will.† Whenever a soul is thus acted upon by grace, he who directs her must teach her the meaning of spiritual consolation and desolation.‡

Spiritual consolation is recognized by the following signs :—The soul, under the action of interior emotions, is on fire with love for God, and can love nothing created save in view of him. Tears flow, stirring up that divine love, whether they flow from grief for sin, or from meditation on the passion, or from any other cause whatever that tends directly to the glory and service of God. We may also give the name, spiritual consolation, to any increase of faith, hope, and charity, and also to every joy which is wont to incite the soul to the meditation of heavenly things, to the desire of salvation, to the possession of rest and peace with God.§

We call spiritual desolation any darkening and

---

* *Director*, n. 2.   † Ibid., c. xxvii, n. 1.
‡ *Exercit. regulæ aliquot—reg.* 3ª.   § Ibid.

disturbance of the mind instigating to low and earthly things; also, every disquietude and agitation or temptation, which moves to distrust concerning salvation, and expels hope and charity, whence the soul finds herself all torpid, lukewarm, sorrowful, and, as it were, separated from her Creator and Lord.* To know, therefore, what side we have to choose, we must examine to what spiritual consolation and peace of mind incline us, when they make themselves felt in the soul; and also to what desolation inclines us. The evil spirit is wont to excite confusion in the soul, to overwhelm it with pusillanimity, sadness, and torpor. The good spirit, on the other hand, brings joy to the soul, and acts upon her, and influences her during consolation.† It is to his voice that we must listen, while closing our ears entirely to the suggestions of the Evil One. When we find ourselves impelled toward the vanities of the world, to the enjoyments of sense, to useless desires, we may be sure that it is the bad spirit who is speaking to us, and we should drive him off with indignation.‡

Another practice that may be followed during an election is that indicated by St. Ignatius under the comparison of a servant who presents to his master several dishes, in order to discover which of them will meet his favor. In the same way,

---

* *Exercit. regulæ aliquot—reg.* 4ª. † *Director.*, c. xxvii, n. 5.
‡ Bona, "Discernment of Spirits," c. vi.

the soul, with profound humility and ardent love, and an immense desire to prove her gratitude to God, offers him at one time this state, and at another that state, carefully noting the one that gives most pleasure to God, and often saying: "Lord, what wilt thou have me do?" She ought to repeat this request, not with her lips only, but with her whole heart.* Among the signs of God's will calling us to the most perfect state, there is this one, which is excellent, namely: when the soul feels that the difficulties of a perfect life, which appear so annoying to others, and formerly seemed so to herself, begin to grow light and pleasant. Another mark is, when thoughts of perfection constantly urge the soul to something better. For Satan, when concealing himself under an appearance of good, may at first hide his stratagems, but he soon appears in his real character and displays his wrath. †

Thus far we have assigned the rules relative to the two first times favorable for choosing a state of the Christian life. If, while the soul is in any of these conditions, she is sufficiently enlightened as to the decision she should come to, and if she is sufficiently firm in her resolve, so that she has no wish for further certainty, she may stop there; but, if the decision is not steady enough, she may pass on to a third time, or to the third state suited to a right election. ‡ This

---

* *Director.*, c. xxvii, n. 6.   † Ibid., n. 7.   ‡ Ibid., c. xxvii, n. 8.

third state differs from the others, inasmuch as in them the will goes first and draws the intellect after it; but in the latter, on the contrary, the intellect has the principal part, and it sets before the will such an array of reasons, that it hurries the will into the adoption of what it judges to be best.*

With regard to this third time, St. Ignatius gives two methods of acting, which we here set before the reader. In both of them, and indeed whenever there is question of choosing a state of life, the soul must be calm and in peace; for, when she is troubled, she cannot make a proper choice.†

During desolation no decision should be made. We should not change our resolutions nor our state of life, but persevere in what was previously determined or decided during moments of spiritual consolation. In desolation we are under the action of the Evil Spirit, and his suggestions cannot lead us to a right and good choice.‡

Here now is the first method for choosing a state when the soul is in peace. We give it in an abridged form, since what we have hitherto said enables us to dispense with details.

The first point is, to place before our minds the state which we intend to embrace.

The second point is, to recall the end of our creation, which is to praise God and save our souls by promoting his glory; then to be indifferent,

---

* *Director.*, c. xxiii, n. 1. † Ibid., c. xxviii, n. 2.
‡ *Exercit. regulæ aliquot—reg.* 5ª.

and ready to adopt whatever may appear best fitted for our own salvation and the glory of God.

Third, to entreat the mercy of God to impel our will in the direction in which we ought in preference to go.

Fourth, to consider the advantages and help which the state offers for salvation and God's glory, and also the difficulties and dangers that are to be met with in it. Consider, likewise, what help and advantages for salvation, as well as obstacles, the opposite state may present.

Fifth, compare the advantages and disadvantages of both sides; listen only to the dictates of reason, set aside all inclinations of corrupt nature, and conclude the election.

Sixth, as soon as the election is over, immediately pray and offer it to God, that he may accept and confirm it, if such be his good pleasure.*

The second method of choosing well contains four rules and one important remark.

The first rule is, take care that your inclination for a state proceed from and have in view God alone.

The second rule. Consider what you would advise a man altogether unknown to you, who would consult you about choosing a state of life, and in whom you would wish no perfection to be wanting. After this consideration, say to yourself: "I would choose what I should advise him."

---

* *Exercit. modus prior electionis.*

The third rule. Ask yourself: "If I were about to die, how would I wish to have decided? It is clear that I should now choose what at the hour of my death I would wish to have done."

The fourth rule. Seriously say to yourself: "When I shall stand before the judgment-seat of God, what shall I wish to have done? That I shall now choose immediately, so that I may appear with greater security before my Judge."

Remark. Having carefully observed these four rules, the election is to be concluded and offered to God for his approval.*

When, in following both of these methods, we obtain the same result, it is a proof that the choice has been well made.† It is good to put in writing the reasons for and against the matters on which we deliberate, because thereby the truth becomes clearer and more striking.‡ These reasons are afterward to be submitted to our spiritual director.

These last two methods given by St. Ignatius afford the surest means of making a right election. If, to the reasons furnished by the intellect for embracing perfection, be added experience of the dangers to be met with in the world, so as to make us sensible that salvation runs great risks there, we can act with much more certainty in our determination.§

---

* *Exerc. modus posterior.* † *Director.*, c. xxxi, n. 1. ‡ Ibid., n. 3
§ Ibid., c. xxviii, nn. 6, 7.

"Yet, while following all these rules, we must not expect," says St. Liguori, "an angel from heaven to come and point out to us the career we have to follow, in order to correspond to God's designs in our regard. It is enough to set before our eyes the state which we think of embracing; afterward we have to reflect on the end at which we aim, and weigh circumstances well."* We should also keep in view what was said in the third chapter of this second section.

---

* Ascetic Works, vol. 3, ed. Castermann.

CHAPTER VI.

HOW TO ACT AFTER AN ELECTION.

First, when a person has come to the conclusion to remain in the world and to content himself with the observance of the commandments, it yet remains for him to deliberate how he shall observe these commandments, and what profession or condition in the world he is to take up and faithfully pursue. This demands careful examination, so that his life may be well regulated.*

When we have to deliberate, not on the choice of a state of life, but on some undertaking, as, for instance, on accepting or refusing some office, we should keep to the rules laid down in the foregoing chapter, taking care always—for this is a capital point—to act in view of God's glory and not for earthly interests.† Who does not deplore the sad neglect of this principle in our days? Passion, human advantages, drive men into careers fraught with danger for salvation, and that for some trifling and perishable gain. Who can tell the amount of evil that flows from such conduct?

---

* *Director.*, c. xxv, n. 8. † Ibid., n. 9.

HOW TO ACT AFTER AN ELECTION. 283

As in the time of St. Gregory, so in our own day there are many avocations which a man can scarcely, or even not at all, take upon himself, without committing sin: "*Sunt pleraque negotia, quæ sine peccatis exhiberi aut vix aut nullatenus possunt.*" (Hom. 24, in Evang.) Therefore, after his return to God, a man must be exceedingly careful not to expose himself anew to anything that would lead him into sin.

When a person has decided to enter the religious state, the next thing to be done is to examine what order should be preferred. Some orders are more given to solitude; others devote themselves very much to the service of their fellowmen. Considering only a person's qualities of mind and body, it is easy to see that one order may be very suitable, and another altogether unsuited.* Above all, no one should enter any order in which religious discipline is not well kept.† St. Liguori, who also gives this counsel, adds that a confessor should consider it his duty not to recommend such an order.‡ "Inquire first," says Lessius, "whether the essential vows are well kept in the order you intend to enter, so that you will find there neither property, nor superfluities, nor too easy communication with the opposite sex.§ Inquire also whether peace and fraternal union reign among the religious." ‖

---

* *Director.*, c. xxxv, n. 4. † Ibid., n. 6.
‡ *Praxis confess.*, n. 92. § Lessius, q. 4, n. 53. ‖ Ibid.

Among fervent communities, the most perfect is to be preferred. To judge of this perfection, one should be acquainted with the teaching of St. Thomas, and know the strength, inclinations, qualities, and talents of the aspirant.* Now, to understand the doctrine of St. Thomas, we must define the various kinds of life that a person may lead in a religious community. There are the active, the contemplative, and the mixed life.

"According to St. Gregory, the active life is: to feed the hungry, to teach the ignorant wisdom, to bring back to humility him whom pride is leading astray, to take care of the sick, give to every one what is profitable for him, and provide for the wants of those intrusted to our charge. The contemplative life retains, indeed, love for God and for our neighbor, but it rests by keeping from exterior activity. Its sole aim is God; outward marks have no charm for it, it tramples all earthly cares under foot, and burns only with ardor to see the face of God." †

The mixed life unites action and contemplation. The active life is good; the contemplative is better; the mixed life, which comprises both, is perfection itself. Jesus Christ, St. John the Baptist, and the apostles, led the mixed life. Our divine Lord spent his nights in prayer and preached during the day.‡ "Works of the active life which

---

* *Director.*, c. xxv, n. 6. † Hom. 2. in Ezech., n. 8.
‡ Corn. à Lapide in Luc. x, 42.

spring from the fulness of contemplation, such as teaching and preaching, are preferable to mere contemplation. It is better to enlighten than to shine only; and it is a nobler kind of life to share with others what we have contemplated, than to confine ourselves to contemplation. Other works of the active life, whose aim is exterior care, such as almsgiving, exercising hospitality and the like, are inferior to works of contemplation, except in cases of extreme need.

" Therefore, religious orders that teach and preach, hold the first rank, and come nearest to the perfection of bishops. Contemplative orders occupy the second place; and those that devote themselves to exterior works are in the third." Such is the teaching of St. Thomas.*

Among communities of the same rank, those have the precedence whose works are noblest, though belonging to the same species as those works of other communities. Thus, in the active life, it is better to ransom captives than to give hospitality or shelter; and in the contemplative life, it is better to pray than to read. Another form of superiority in an order arises from its doing more kinds of work than others, and from its rules affording more efficacious means for the attainment of its end.†

The perfection of an order is not always a pledge of its security. The contemplative life,

---

* Div. Th., 2, 2, q. 188, a. 6. † Ibid.

though less perfect than the mixed, is, nevertheless, safer. Salvation is there surrounded with greater protection.*

Cloistered houses have the immense advantage of shutting out all occasion of sin that is to be found in the world. Those who, in the world, have learned to know their weakness, do well in preferring them as their place of rest, and as a port after shipwreck. The approbation of the Church is the basis, the support, and the strength of religious societies. Happy the associations that have received this blessing, the value of which cannot be too highly esteemed! When, in accordance with the rules we have given, a person has chosen the order in which he is to pass his days, he must still be on his guard against inconstancy and negligence in following his vocation. "He who has made a good choice," says St. Ignatius, "has no reason to recall it, but should endeavor to strengthen himself in it more and more."† To give up a greater good is, according to St. Thomas, an act of imprudence. A salutary project which has been determined on, cannot be abandoned without some defect and error on the part of reason, from the fact that it rejects what it had deliberately accepted.‡

To renounce the religious life after a prudent

---

* Gautrelet, vol. 2, page 180; Suar., Tract. 9, lib. 1, c. vi, n. 29, *De varietate religionum.*
† *Exercit., introd. ad eligend., etc., quartum.*
‡ Div. Th. 2, 2, q. 53, a. 5.

determination to embrace it, is to rob one's self of the greatest good.

It is a duty to respect all the serious impediments that we have enumerated; but it is an error, or at least a weakness, to stop at obstacles arising from unjust opposition on the part of parents, from excessive natural affection, from a groundless fear of not persevering, or of falling into greater sins in the religious state; or, finally, from a misconceived humility that, on account of past sins, makes a person deem himself unworthy of the state of perfection. We should, therefore, rise up bravely against obstacles coming from men, or from our own want of courage. If the combat terrifies us, let the reward that is in store for us stimulate our ardor.

"When the hour has come to carry out our vocation to the state of perfection, a difficulty sometimes arises. In things painful to nature, human weakness keeps us back as much as possible. It seeks reasons to justify its delays and to deceive itself. 'The grace of the Holy Ghost knows nothing of such delays,' says St. Ambrose. We should follow the example of the apostles, who abandoned directly their nets and their relations. We should reason in this way: 'If I am one day to embrace perfection, why not do it now? If I do not take it up immediately, perhaps I shall never do so. For, at present, I am under the influence of grace, I feel its assistance: that grace may very easily grow weak, and then it would be more difficult for me to resist nature and the Evil Spirit.'"* But there are some whom God really calls to the path of Christian perfection, and yet there are excusable hindrances in their way. For instance, a young man needs to recruit his health; a young woman is only eighteen years of age, and she must wait until her twenty-first year, because the convent that she intends to enter will not accept her before she is of age, as her parents now refuse their consent. Or again, it is a young man who cannot leave his parents in their present extreme need. In cases of this kind, here is the advice given by St. Liguori:—

"He who is absolutely forced to wait, should spare no pains, in order to preserve his vocation, since it is the richest treasure he can own. There are three means to preserve a vocation: discretion, prayer, and recollection. Generally speaking, one's own vocation should be kept secret, and made known to no one except a confessor; for people of the world usually make no scruple about telling young persons called to the religious state that God can be served in all conditions of life, even amid the seductions of the world; and, what is most astonishing," says the holy doctor, "is that such remarks come from priests, and at times even from religious. Hence, my dear brother, if God inspires you to give up

---

* *Director.*, c. xxv, n. 7.

the world, take care not to make it known to your parents. Be satisfied with the blessing of the Lord. For the same reason do not let your friends know your vocation, because they would make no difficulty about inducing you to give it up, or at least about publishing your secret, which would thus come to the knowledge of your parents."*

Some persons may here say that these words of the learned and illustrious bishop tend to lessen the confidence of children in their parents. Indeed this confidence would be unlimited if parents knew all their duties, and sufficiently appreciated the state of perfection to second their children's desire to embrace it. But experience proves too well that such is not the case. To set limits, therefore, to the confidence of children, is only to apply the words of the Holy Ghost: "We ought to obey God rather than men." (Acts v, 29.) As it is important to conceal our vocation from those who might thwart it, so it is good to make it known to a man of God, who has, as Suarez requires, right notions on the religious life. How many souls have foregone the religious state, because they considered the gates of religion closed forever against them on account of their slender instruction or temporal means! They would have been readily admitted, had they but applied for information to the charity of some virtuous

---

*Ascetic Works: "The Choice of a State." Ed. Castermann, vol. 3, p. 415.

priest. There are many mansions in the house of the Lord. The poor and the ignorant can find place in it, if they only go to a zealous confessor who will prepare it for them.

"Rest assured," continues St. Liguori, "that without prayer you will scarcely preserve a religious vocation. Therefore do not fail to pray. Pay likewise every day a visit to the Blessed Sacrament and to our Lady, to beg the grace of continuing in your vocation."

The holy doctor next recommends frequentation of the sacraments, and then he adds: "All your prayers to Jesus and Mary, and particularly at communion, must have for object to obtain perseverance." Finally, he says: "It is necessary to live in retirement and recollection. But this is out of the question, if you do not keep away from the diversions of the world. What is required to destroy a vocation in the world? Almost nothing: one day of amusement, a little vexation not properly borne,—things of this kind are sometimes enough to put to flight all our resolutions to give ourselves wholly to God But whosoever allows himself to be carried away by worldly enjoyments, will infallibly lose his vocation. How many, from want of recollection and of keeping away from the world, lost, first, their vocation, and, next, their immortal souls!"*

---

*Ascetic Works: "The Choice of a State." Ed. Castermann, vol. 3, p. 422.

Conclusion.

In the second part of this book we have furnished rules for the choice of a state of life; in the first, we attempted to draw out an exact idea of the various states of the Christian life. Our task is therefore at an end. Blessed be God who gave us time and strength to begin it and bring it to a close. O Lord! may this humble work promote thy glory! We ask this of thee through Mary, thy divine mother, and our mother also. May all who shall read these pages be enlightened by thy light and touched by thy grace, so that they may devote to thy service, every one in his way, the life which they hold from thee! Holy doctors! whose doctrine we have borrowed, fertilize by your protection the instruction which you have given us. May it be understood by all whom the prejudices of the world deceive and lead astray!

PRAYERS.

"I exhort you to say, during nine days, the following prayer," said St. Liguori to a young woman who consulted him on her vocation:—

"'O Lord Jesus Christ, who didst die to save me! I beseech thee, by the merits of thy blood, to give me the light and strength that I need, in order to choose the state which shall be most conducive to my salvation.

"'And thou, O my loving mother, Mary ever Virgin! obtain for me this grace through thy powerful intercession.'"*

"I wish you," wrote the same holy doctor to a young man,—"I wish you to say this short prayer which I send you:—

"'O my God! I am a wretched creature, that in past times has despised thee. To-day, however, I esteem and love thee above all things, and I wish never more to love any one or any thing but thee. Thou wishest to have me wholly for thyself, and I wish to belong altogether to thee. Speak, O Lord! thy servant heareth. Make known to me what thou askest of me: my wish is to conform entirely to thy divine will. Especially do I beg of thee to let me know in what state thou willest that I should serve thee.'"†

Lastly, St. Liguori gives this advice to souls that are called to the religious state: "In all your prayers, at all your communions, you should remember to renew to God the offering of yourselves, saying:—

"'Here I am, O Lord! I no longer belong to myself: I am wholly thine. I have already given myself to thee, and I now give myself to thee again. Deign to accept my offering, give me strength to be faithful to thee, and to retire as soon as possible into thy holy house.'"‡

---

* Ascetic Works, ed. Castermann, vol. 3, pp. 511, 512.
† Ibid., p. 309. ‡ Ibid., p. 422.

www.ingramcontent.com/pod-product-compliance
Lightning Source LLC
Chambersburg PA
CBHW030815230426
43667CB00008B/1229